THEIR GOD
— IS SO —
BIG

Teaching Sunday School to young children

by Stephanie Carmichael

❧ MATTHIAS MEDIA

For

Mum and Dad

Ian, Lauren and Glen

Their God is so Big © Matthias Media, 2000

Published in Australia by:
Matthias Media
PO Box 225, Kingsford NSW 2032
ph +61-(0)2 9663 1478
fax +61-(0)2 9662 4289
email: info@matthiasmedia.com.au
Internet: www.matthiasmedia.com.au
(St Matthias Press Ltd ACN 067 558 365)

Distributed in the U.K. by:
The Good Book Company
Elm House,
37 Elm Road, New Malden,
Surrey KT3 3HB
ph (020) 8942 0880
email: admin@thegoodbook.co.uk

Distributed in South Africa by:
Christian Book Discounters
ph (021) 685 3663
email: peter@christianbooks.co.za

ISBN 1 876326 27 1

Design and typesetting by Joy Lankshear Design Pty Ltd

Illustrated by Lauren Carmichael, Glen Carmichael, Alex Cole,
Nigel Hill and Melissa Wright

Contents

Introduction

About this book

I hold Sunday School teachers in the highest regard. It is a wonderful and important ministry, and rarely an easy one. It is about serving children who are not always a pleasure to teach, who may have tantrums, conduct impromptu paper throwing competitions, or just be rude. On the other hand, it is about serving children who are fragile people in a sinful world and need more than anything to be well-taught in the holy Scriptures, which are able to make them wise for salvation through faith in Christ Jesus (2 Tim 3:15).

We can't wait until children grow up before we teach them about God. Children go to school to learn how to read, write and count; they also need to learn how to live, according to the intentions of our Creator. Many who have become Christians in adulthood are saddened by the fact that they didn't come into a relationship with God earlier, and so could have avoided years of uncertainty, insecurity and doubt.

I will not spend much time saying how worthwhile and important Sunday School teaching is. I assume that you already think this way if you are reading this book.

This book is aimed at teachers of young children. To have covered children of all ages I would have ended up writing an epic. Rather than presenting you with a paperweight, I thought it more valuable to address an age range that is often overlooked. Even if you are teaching older children, it's helpful for you to consider these early years and how children develop concepts of God.

The book is designed to be used in three ways:

- as a manual for the Sunday School teacher; Part 1 explains the basic practicalities of teaching a Sunday School class; Part 2 also contains valuable resources and suggestions for teachers.
- as a course-book for a teacher training course; there is an outline of a teacher training course in chapter 13 and there are training exercises/questions throughout the book for personal reflection or group discussion.
- as a resource for Sunday School co-ordinators/superintendents. Part 2 is especially for you!

Throughout the book, and especially in Part 1, there are various practical exercises. These are called 'think and pray' or 'challenge and change' or 'think and do', or some similar title. They are fairly straightforward and require little further explanation, except to note that the exercises entitled 'challenge and change' are especially aimed at those who are already teaching a Sunday School class.

A personal note...

I started writing this book years ago, and it has only been a publisher's deadline that has made me finish it. A constant thought—"but I still have more to learn"—has always kept me from thinking that the manuscript is finished. Only recently, I had a Sunday School teaching experience that was less than ideal, and I couldn't help saying to myself, "And you're writing a book about teaching Sunday School!" It was a humbling experience, reminding me that as teachers we are still learners; we can never know it all nor give the perfect lesson. And the fact that we teach children, who are the greatest variable of all, means that we can never predict exactly how things are going to go.

So it is with a humble heart that I bring this book to you. It contains what I have learnt thus far in my teaching journey, and I hope it can be of help to you. I don't look upon myself as having all the answers, but I hope that you will find help and encouragement in the pages that follow.

My prayer is that God will keep teaching us all about himself, about children and about teaching—and indeed that he will keep helping us to teach children about God.

Stephanie Carmichael
OCTOBER, 2000

Part 1

Basic skills of Sunday School teaching

Chapter 1

The Sunday School Teacher

In this chapter

1. Characteristics of a Sunday School teacher
2. The model of the Apostle Paul
3. Some words of advice for new teachers
4. For experienced teachers
5. For those teaching in a team

1. Characteristics of a Sunday School teacher

As Sunday School teachers, we must never lose sight of the fact that our role is very important. Teaching **anybody** the Word of God is an important ministry (1 Tim 5:17). Teaching children about God is just as significant—remember that Jesus rebuked his disciples when they made the mistake of regarding children as less important than adults in ministry terms (Matt 19:13-14).

Indeed, the seriousness of teaching children is probably greater in some respects because of the duty of care involved. Children are very trusting. Young children, in particular, believe what adults tell them. We need to be worthy of that trust by teaching the Bible carefully and not leading them into error or misunderstanding. We have both a privilege and a responsibility: a privilege to be able to tell them about God and his Word, and a responsibility to teach them faithfully.

James tells us that teachers will be judged more strictly (Jas 3:1), presumably because of the potential damage they can do to the spiritual lives of those they teach. I can only think that James would reserve the strongest warning for teachers of those who can be most easily led astray—young children.

▲ ● ■
THINK

The qualifications for elders, overseers and deacons which Scripture sets out in passages such as 1 Timothy 3 and Titus 1 tell us a great deal about the sort of people Sunday School teachers should be. Read through the qualities required of overseers and deacons in 1 Timothy 3:1-13.

a. Which do you think would be important qualities to have as a Sunday School teacher?

b. Are there any which you consider inapplicable?

At the end of this chapter, we will work through part of 1 Thessalonians, as an example of the characteristics of a godly ministry relationship. But let me give you a summary of what makes for a good Sunday School teacher.

a. A godly model

Sunday School teachers teach through their lives and not just their words.

- As a Sunday School teacher, you are a significant adult in the lives of the children in your class. Children look to significant adults as models, and learn appropriate behaviour from them.
- The children will look to you for a living example of what it means to be a Christian—whether you want that or not. So make sure that you set a godly example: "set an example for the believers in speech, in life, in love, in faith and in purity" (1 Tim 4:12).
- An apt description of the example we should be setting is Galatians 5:22-23: "…the fruit of the Spirit is love, joy, peace, patience, kindness, goodness, faithfulness, gentleness and self-control".

b. Committed

- One of the key aspects of the role of Sunday School teaching is commitment. You need to be committed to the ministry, the children and the team of teachers you are working with. Children quickly pick up an idea of how much you care for them by seeing how committed you are to teaching them well every week.
- The ministry of Sunday School is worth being committed to—it can be the beginning of a life of faith, and as such is a precious and valuable opportunity.
- Show this commitment by being punctual, by watching how late you stay up on Saturday night, and by avoiding any other commitments which may mean missing a week of Sunday School.
- It is best if you can view teaching as a long-term commitment rather than short-term. In one year you get to know your class and the children build a relationship with you. You will be much more effective in your teaching in your second and third years of teaching the same children.

c. Caring

- We're telling the children about God's love and the importance of loving others; thus we must show this love to them.
- Children can sense whether you are showing genuine care and interest.
- Here are some practical ways of showing you care:
  - Take an interest in the children's interests (remember who loves cricket and who likes soccer). Initiate conversations about their interests.
  - Remember events that are important to children (e.g. birthdays). If a child tells you about a forthcoming event, then remember to ask them about it. They will be delighted that you remembered.
  - If possible, visit them at home (after arranging it with their parents of course).

- Remember that some children may have emotional problems, e.g. a family break-up, being bullied at school, failing at school, and so on. Children are very sensitive emotionally, and we need to provide them with a positive, caring environment.

d. Prepared

- Preparation is very important for the effectiveness of a lesson.
- Set aside adequate time during the week to do preparation.
- Ensure that you are ready for the children when they arrive. Don't be caught out—children know when you are not prepared. It is important to them to know that they are important to you and worth preparing for.

e. Enthusiastic

- Enthusiasm is contagious.
- We should be enthusiastic about God's Word and the ministry of Sunday School teaching: "Never be lacking in zeal, but keep your spiritual fervour, serving the Lord" (Rom 12:11).

f. Prayerful

- All Christian ministry should be surrounded with prayer.
- It is God who helps us in our teaching and we should be relying on him.
- Pray for your own faithfulness and teaching, and pray for your children and their understanding. In the end, it is only the work of the Holy Spirit which can make God's light shine in the hearts of the children you teach (2 Cor 4:6).

▲ ● ■
THINK AND PRAY

Read back over this section describing the qualities of a Sunday School teacher. Write down any areas of your life that you have been challenged about. Pray for God's help to change and continue to be challenged.

2. The model of the Apostle Paul

Just as we need to be a model to the children, so we can learn from the good example of other ministers of the gospel. Let's take a look at one such model now.

1 Thessalonians gives us an insight into the relationship between the Apostle Paul and the Christians he is committed to caring for at Thessalonica. Paul regards the Thessalonians as his spiritual children—he suggests that he is like a mother and a father to them (2:7,11).

What can we learn from Paul about caring for 'young' Christians?

What are some of the characteristics we see in Paul that we should aim for as teachers of children? Let's look at 1 Thessalonians 2:17–3:13.

> [17] But, brothers, when we were torn away from you for a short time (in person, not in thought), out of our intense longing we made every effort to see you. [18] For we wanted to come to you—certainly I, Paul, did, again and again—but Satan stopped us. [19] For what is our hope, our joy, or the crown in which we will glory in the presence of our Lord Jesus when he comes? Is it not you? [20] Indeed, you are our glory and joy.
>
> 3 [1] So when we could stand it no longer, we thought it best to be left by ourselves in Athens. [2] We sent Timothy, who is our brother and God's fellow-worker in spreading the gospel of Christ, to strengthen and encourage you in your faith, [3] so that no-one would be unsettled by these trials. You know quite well that we were destined for them. [4] In fact, when we were with you, we kept telling you that we would be persecuted. And it turned out that way, as you well know. [5] For this reason, when I could stand it no longer, I sent to find out about your faith. I was afraid that in some way the tempter might have tempted you and our efforts might have been useless.
>
> [6] But Timothy has just now come to us from you and has brought good news about your faith and love. He has told us that you always have pleasant memories of us and that you long to see us, just as we also long to see you. [7] Therefore, brothers, in all our distress and persecution we were encouraged about you because of your faith. [8] For now we really live, since you are standing firm in the Lord. [9] How can we thank God enough for you in return for all the joy we have in the presence of our God because of you? [10] Night and day we pray most earnestly that we may see you again and supply what is lacking in your faith.
>
> [11] Now may our God and Father himself and our Lord Jesus clear the way for us to come to you. [12] May the Lord make your love increase and overflow for each other and for everyone else, just as ours does for you. [13] May he strengthen your hearts so that you will be blameless and holy in the presence of our God and Father when our Lord Jesus comes with all his holy ones.

Let's note a few points from this.

Firstly, look at the end of the quoted passage to see the **goal** towards which Paul is striving. That's what we're working towards in Sunday School as well. We're not just a childminding service; we want to see children grow in the Lord so that they will be "blameless and holy in the presence of God our Father" on the last day when Jesus returns. We must never lose sight of this big picture. We're working towards a heavenly goal.

Secondly, Paul **loves** being with them, because he **loves to minister** to them (2:17, 3:10). He hates to be separated from them. He does everything he can to see them again—and when he can't, he sacrifices some of his own comforts by sending Timothy (3:1,2).

Will you hate to be apart from your kids—to miss Sunday School?

Will you look forward every week to seeing the kids again in order to minister to them? Will you be truly concerned about them (3:5) and pray for them between seeing them (3:10)? If, despite your longing to be there, you can't get to Sunday School, will you make sure you send a trusted replacement (3:2)?

In other words, will you love the kids with an increasing love that overflows (3:12)? Will you love them so much that they experience your love and they look forward to seeing you again each week (3:6) and many years from now will have "pleasant memories" of you?

It's a daunting example to follow. How do you get that sort of love and that sort of commitment? When Sunday School is tiring, frustrating, or discouraging, and a seemingly relentless grind week-by-week, how do you muster the love of which Paul speaks?

Two answers flow from the passage.

Firstly, since God is the one who makes people abound in love, we should pray for it (3:12). This type of love and commitment is not natural; it is a fruit of God's Spirit. Love, joy, peace, patience, kindness, goodness, faithfulness, gentleness and self-control—these are the things you need to keep going week by week. But remember, they come from the grace of God. So pray.

Secondly, we need to lift our eyes to heaven. For how does Paul view these people? As a burden? As a heavy responsibility? No. As his glory and joy, because on the last day, when they are all together in the presence of God, they will be like crowns of glory to him (2:19-20). Because Paul's perspective is heavenly and eternal, he can hardly find the words to thank God enough for the joy they give him (3:9).

Will some of the children in your Sunday School class persevere to the last day, partly because of your ministry to them? Will they be your crown in which you glory in the very presence of the Lord Jesus? Having this mindset will change forever your attitude to the weekly routine of teaching.

▲ ● ■

THINK AND PRAY

Look back over the passage from 1 Thessalonians.

a. What does Paul say about Satan (or 'the tempter')?

b. How should this motivate us in our care for children, and our prayers?

c. Is your thinking about life and Christian ministry dominated by God's kingdom and the return of Jesus (as Paul's seems to be)? What things do dominate your thinking? Pray that God would transform your mind.

d. Paul overflows with thankfulness. Spend some time thanking God for each of the children in your care, and for the opportunity to teach them.

3. Some words of advice for new teachers

Let me give a few special words of advice for new teachers who may feel particularly daunted by the task they are taking on.

- Teachers are learners—there's always something for us all to learn. Every teacher, at some point, is at the beginning of the learning curve. So don't get discouraged; remember that mistakes happen to everyone.
- Be prepared to be flexible—when teaching children there are so many variables that are out of our control; e.g. the weather, the mood of the children, or a child arriving in tears. You need to be flexible and bounce back, remembering that you usually can't predict or control what 'variables' you will be faced with. Don't take it as a personal failure if your lesson doesn't go perfectly to plan.
- Confidence takes time to develop—don't expect too much too soon.
- Willingness is a key element of good teaching. You can't begin teaching as an experienced expert, but if you're willing to have a go and learn then you're more than half-way there. Enthusiasm, eagerness and commitment to both God and the children are more important than experience.

- Be realistic—begin with well thought out lesson plans. The more prepared you are, especially in your first few lessons, the better you will cope with the unexpected. In your early lessons use simple, easy-to-use visual aids and hassle-free activities.
- Expect respect—don't let the children walk all over you. You are the teacher, and what you say goes! So look and act like you are in control, even if you are shaking in your boots.
- Ask for God's help and wisdom. The marvellous thing about any ministry is that God uses our often weak and faltering efforts to do his work.

4. For experienced teachers

All teachers are learners. Regardless of how long we've been teaching for, we still have things to learn. This means that we need to have a teachable spirit, to be willing to change and to try new ideas.

Experienced teachers are a great asset to any Sunday School because they add stability. You can be an encouragement and example to new teachers. You are also in a position to develop close relationships with the children in your class.

5. For those teaching in a team

Many of us have the opportunity of teaching in a team. It is wonderful to have the support and help that can come from two or more teachers working together. Here are some considerations:

- Don't slacken in your commitment to Sunday School because there is more than one teacher.
- Spend time together establishing guidelines for the class routine, discipline, the syllabus and individual teacher's responsibilities. This is important for consistency.
- Aim to encourage and support each other (in both words and actions). Be committed to helping each other and supporting each other through prayer.
- You can divide the workload among a team of teachers in a number of ways. Choose which one (or combination) suits your situation best:

    i. Each week one member of the team is responsible for preparing and presenting the entire lesson, with the other teachers giving assistance when appropriate. This means that the main message of the lesson is clearly presented and reinforced throughout the lesson.
    ii. A different teacher is responsible for the story each week and that teacher assigns other team members to do other parts of the

lesson. This means that the teacher responsible for the story is the one in charge that week.

iii. One teacher takes on the role of leader for the whole year. He/she is the overall coordinator of the lesson every week, i.e. introduces each part of the lesson and the teacher responsible for it; is the main disciplinarian; remembers any announcements that need to be made, and so on. This way of running a class means that the children know who is in control and they develop a rapport with the 'leader'.

iv. The teachers are assigned responsibility each week for one part of the lesson. So one week a teacher might prepare the craft and the next week he/she prepares the story. There needs to be close communication between team members so that the main message is the same in each part of the lesson that day. There also needs to be effective coordination so that each part of the lesson is prepared each week.

v. Similar to above, the teachers assume responsibility each week for the same part of the lesson (i.e. story, craft, memory verse/ action rhyme, prayer). This is good for consistency and ensuring that there is sufficient variety each week (knowing what they prepared the week before). It does mean that some might have a greater workload than others.

In summary, when teaching in a team, there needs to be:
· communication—between teachers
· commitment—to each other and the class
· control—one teacher needs to be clearly in control each week
· consistency—in routines and class management
· coordination—so that the 'team' works as a team

a. If you are a new teacher, pray about the points listed above, especially for God's help in developing confidence and wisdom.

PRAY

b. If you have taught Sunday School before, pray that you might be a godly model (modelling how to teach Sunday School to new teachers, and modelling a godly way of life to your class). Pray for the humility to keep learning and growing in your teaching skills.

c. If you are teaching in a team, pray for your fellow teachers. Pray that you will be able to work as a team, supporting each other. Pray for wisdom in organization and class management.

Chapter 2
Understanding children

In this chapter

1. Children as individuals
2. Ages and stages
3. Two-year-olds
4. Pre-school children (3-4 years)
5. Infants children (5-7 years)

Children are not miniature adults. It is sometimes easy to view them as such, but we are mistaken when we do. Children are children. It takes time to get to know what children are like—how they live and learn, and how they view the world. If you have had little contact with children it can be difficult to make the adjustment from an adult's perspective to that of a child.

If we want to teach children about God, then we certainly need to spend time getting to know about children and especially the age group we are going to teach.

1. Children as individuals

Children are all different. It sounds obvious, and in many ways it is; yet it is easy to forget. We know that children look different—that's the obvious part. And yet we can too easily overlook the fact that their personalities, abilities, likes and dislikes vary enormously.

Later in this chapter I have described the characteristics of each age group. This will be a helpful guide, and you will be wise to keep your expectations in line with the general characteristics of the age group that you are teaching. At the same time, we need to remember that there may be widely differing abilities within each class. Some of the differences that may be apparent include:

- self-image and level of confidence
- physical abilities
- ability to listen, concentrate, understand and remember
- speed in doing tasks
- accuracy and desire to be accurate
- in younger children, their ability to use paste, scissors, pencils
- in older children, their reading, writing and spelling skills

And the list could go on.

We will also encounter a variety of personalities in any one age group of children. Their likes and dislikes will differ, sometimes greatly. One child's idea of fun may be running around outside kicking a ball, while for another child it may be sitting in a corner with a book or a puzzle. We cannot assume that all children will get the same level of enjoyment from an activity.

So a group of children should be viewed as a group of individuals, each with their own personalities, abilities, likes and dislikes. Aim to get to know each child well, discovering their uniqueness and learning how to love them. It takes time, and in some cases effort, but it is a fundamental part of caring for our children and being able to teach them God's Word effectively. The following information could be recorded for each child to assist you in getting to know them.

Name: _____

Address: _____

_____

_____

_____

Parents names: _____

_____

Birth date: /   /   _____

Special interests or hobbies: _____

_____

_____

Preferred topics of conversation: _____

_____

_____

_____

Any special problems: _____

_____

_____

Any special needs: _____

_____

_____

2. Ages and stages

a. A reference guide to ages covered in this book

Two-year-olds: don't go to pre-school but may go to long day care centres.

Three-year-olds: children must have turned three before they are accepted at pre-school. If children commence pre-school while they are three they usually spend two years there.

Four-year-olds: many four-year-olds go to pre-school. Children need to be at least four and a half before they can commence school.

Five-year-olds: the majority of children are either five or nearly five when they begin school.

Five to seven years old: these children are at infants school. The three years spent at infants school are—
Kindergarten/Reception
Year 1 (or 1st class)
Year 2 (or 2nd class)

(I realise that many children are turning eight in Year 2, but for the purposes of this book I have called infants children five to seven years.)

b. Characteristics of each age group

The following general characteristics of different age groups should help you to get a rough feel for the children in your care. These characteristics are listed with implications for us as teachers. You may only want to read the section relevant to your class's age range. However, it would be helpful for you to read the characteristics of each age group so that you know where they have come from and where they are heading. Also, within one age range, you will have a variety of differences and some children may well fit into the age bracket above or below their class.

3. Two-year-olds

Physically active
They need 'active' activities and cannot sit still for long.

Very short attention span
You will need to alternate between active and passive activities. Their concentration span is so short that you may need to capture their attention or give them a little break with such things as making their fingers move in different ways (march, walk, dance), or putting their hands on their knees or shoulders. Have a few finger games, songs and activities up your sleeve in case you need them.

Tire easily
Another reason to alternate active and passive activities.

Self-centred
They are at the centre of their own little worlds, and tend to think that they should have you to themselves. In the event of the birth of a baby brother or sister, be extra sensitive to that child. They are suddenly not the centre of attention at home and may react in some way. Make them feel loved and special.

Enjoy and need repetition
For instance, they enjoy hearing nursery rhymes and their favourite books over and over again. Repeat the main message of the story often while talking to them, doing the activity, or playing with them.

Prefer routine
The children need the security of a familiar routine (this has a calming effect).

Need your attention and help
Learn to work with the children, helping them in their tasks rather than expecting them to do an activity alone. Be well prepared so that you can give your full attention to the children.

Should not be hurried
Be flexible and don't pressurise them. Be well organised so that there is a calm, ordered environment.

Need clear directions
When giving instructions, ensure that you have their full attention and give clear instructions, one step at a time. However, you can't give this age group a list of instructions and expect them to remember—it is preferable to give the children one instruction at a time, and then have them follow your instruction before giving them the next one.

Need a controlled environment
When doing an activity, give the children only one thing to do at a time (i.e. just colouring or pasting) so that you can keep control. If an activity requires a few different tasks, then have everyone doing one thing at a time together (e.g. everyone pasting, then put the glue away, then bring the crayons out and everyone 'colouring', i.e. scribbling).

Curious
They are very curious and love asking "What's that?"

Like talking about themselves
Be warned: children will often interrupt you while you are telling the story. It may be more satisfactory to tell the story to children in groups of two or three at a time rather than trying to speak to them as a large group.

Limited in small muscle tasks
Two-year-olds will vary in their abilities, but most are not yet past scribbling.

Independent
They like to do things themselves even though they may not be able to.

A limited vocabulary
Some are very vocal while others (especially boys) may not talk much. They can usually understand more than they can express.

Play by themselves and are not friendly sharers
Even in a group they tend to play beside each other rather than together.

Tantrums
Tantrums are quite common (and normal) as an attempt to exert independence. Don't let the children manipulate you through their behaviour. You need to be firm and loving. In the case of attention-seeking tantrums, it may be best to minimise the attention which they receive at that time.

Sometimes aggressive

Two-year-olds may hit or bite other children. Try to avoid situations that bring about frustration and anti-social behaviour. Patiently and consistently teach the children to share and be kind to each other.

Need security

They may have a security blanket and may feel afraid or insecure easily. Some will find it difficult to leave their parents. Don't bring attention to the shy, insecure child or force them into doing things. Try to make them feel loved and secure. Gradually encourage them to be more involved.

Often say 'no'

It is preferable to give two-year-olds a choice rather than asking a yes/no question, unless you are happy to get the answer 'no'.

Unaware of dangers

Two-year-olds often do not understand the consequences of their actions. Always be aware of the safety of the children. Keep scissors and other dangerous implements out of their reach at all times (unless in your hands). Never let the children out of the cubicle/class space unless accompanied by a teacher. Remember that many two-year-olds are proficient climbers (and acrobats).

Toilet training

Some of the children will not be toilet-trained, or are learning to be trained. Get to know where each child is at, so that you can be prepared! Notice the bags which accompany each child so that you know who has what provisions.

Love to explore

They are active learners and spend their days exploring their world, making new discoveries and learning about the world they live in. They are not born with knowledge and experience—it is learned, and two-year-olds are busily learning all they can.

Imitate adults

They enjoy doing things alongside adults and feeling as if they are helping (e.g. helping Mum or Dad with some household chore). If they want to help, try to encourage this, but you will need to be patient as their help can sometimes be unhelpful!

Play imaginatively

Their lives are full of imagination. Their soft toys are real to them and often the distinction between reality and fantasy is blurred.

Emotionally fragile
Think of how easily a child can cry or laugh or giggle. Just as they are developing physically and mentally, so they are developing emotionally. Thus it's important to be loving, have a calm atmosphere, provide them with routine, and keep their lives as stress-free as possible.

Physically...
- they can scribble, plonk paper on paste
- they can climb (some are quite proficient) and run
- they are learning to jump
- they can't do things like skipping or hopping

4. Pre-school children (3-4 years)

Love listening to stories
They love stories and being read to. They also enjoy watching puppets. Many stories they listen to at this age are fairy tales, so it's important to emphasise that the Bible is true and really happened.

Creative and imaginative
They have a rich fantasy world complete with monsters, dinosaurs, fairies, and all manner of creatures and characters.

Self-centred
Their world is gradually expanding (e.g. attending pre-school) and they are becoming more aware of other people. However, they still are quite self-centred. Try to encourage an awareness of others and how others feel. Individual craft activities are preferable to group activities.

They will often interrupt the story with their own stories about themselves and their families. Give them an opportunity to share in a structured environment (so they don't all talk at once), e.g. news time, discussion after story, and so on. Even so, some will find it difficult to listen and be interested in others without talking themselves.

Limited experience and vocabulary
Use their vocabulary, i.e. the words that they use and understand. Use the known to describe the unknown (e.g. a desert is a place like a beach with lots of sand but no water).

Limited ability to understand
It is important to teach stories within their ability to understand, and to keep stories and concepts simple. In simplifying a Bible story, never distort it and don't teach them anything that will have to be unlearnt at a later date.

Think in concrete terms
Their thinking is very much at a concrete stage, so try to avoid abstract concepts. It is helpful to accompany stories with something visual (i.e. visual aids).

Short attention span
Don't expect them to sit and listen for too long. They need a variety of activities requiring different levels of concentration (i.e. vary active and passive activities). Order your activities carefully so that children are prepared for key concentration times (e.g. the story) and are able to listen effectively when you want them to. They are easily distracted, so be aware of potential distractions, and minimise them. Remember to be brief and to the point.

Enjoy and need repetition
Repetition is important for this age group so don't be afraid to be repetitive. Reinforce the main message in as many ways as possible, e.g. story, craft, discussion. Remember that young children don't equate repetition with boredom.

Need to feel secure
These children can have a range of fears and insecurities beyond themselves, e.g. many children will be scared of the dark, dogs or thunder. Be sensitive to their insecurities, and aim to create a loving environment and a calm atmosphere. Don't bring attention to the shy or insecure child, nor force them to do things.
    The security of a familiar routine is important. Be organised so as to avoid confusion and be seen to be firmly in control.

Enthusiastic about things they enjoy
Present things in a fun, enjoyable way and they will be 'all ears'.

Learn by seeing and doing, not just hearing
We need to use as many of their senses as possible when teaching them. They learn through all their senses, and they will learn best if they are seeing as well as hearing. This is one reason why visual aids are important.

Very active
They will wriggle and squirm, and need active times to release energy. Don't get angry with them for being active, i.e. for being typical pre-schoolers. Rather, cater for their needs. Also remember that they tire easily.

Need clear directions
Don't expect them to remember a list of instructions. They need to be given clear directions, one step at a time (and then they follow those instructions before moving on). Make sure that you have their full attention!

Need consistent discipline and control
Give the children only one thing to do at a time, thus making it easier to keep control (i.e. if an activity requires a few different tasks, have everyone doing one thing at a time together). Set clear limits within which they must behave—be consistent and fair.

Limited in small muscle tasks
Be prepared for a range of drawing, pasting and cutting abilities. Think carefully about the suitability of activities, the time they will take and the amount of teacher involvement required. Don't give the children an activity involving small muscle tasks assuming that all the children will be able to cope. Limit the use of scissors, as they can be dangerous even in the hands of those who can use them.

Physically...
- they can do the following small muscle tasks with varying ability: drawing, colouring in, pasting
- their ability to use scissors varies
- some are learning how to write their name (some can write more)
- they love making things with junk and tape or paste
- their gross motor skills include running, jumping and dancing
- they are learning to hop and skip

5. Infants children (5-7 years)

Learning to read
Their ability will vary, as they all learn at different rates. Don't assume that they can all read. Get to know the ability levels in your class and keep any reading material simple.

Learning to write
Again, their ability will vary. The older children will be able to copy or trace large print. It is important to get to know the ability levels in your class so that you are only expecting them to do what they are capable of. Keep writing to a minimum, as it is slow and spelling will be poor. Remember to only use lower case (i.e. girl not GIRL).

Developing skills in small muscle tasks
Skills will vary; e.g. ability to use scissors and colour in. Some will have a reasonable degree of accuracy while others may appear clumsy. Simplify tasks for children who are weaker in these skills to avoid frustration and feelings of inadequacy.

Short attention span
It is often surprising how short their attention span can be. Just

because they sit at desks at school doesn't mean that they can sit for long periods. So make the most of key concentration times. This age group are active and need opportunities to wriggle and squirm—that is, provide them with opportunities when you want them to wriggle!

Experience and environment widening

Being at school means that their world has expanded somewhat. They are meeting a range of new people from backgrounds different from their own. They are learning new things, experiencing new things and going to new places. They are becoming more aware of others and less self-centred.

Need variety

Variety is important, especially between active and passive activities. Also aim for variety in craft activities (don't have the same type of activity each week—try 3D craft sometimes), and variety in presentation (e.g. visual aids—try puppets and models).

Limited vocabulary

Even though many of these children are reading and writing, their vocabulary is still limited. Try to use simple vocabulary, particularly when explaining difficult concepts.

Think in concrete terms

They are still thinking on a concrete level, so you need to explain things on a concrete level. Limit abstract concepts, use visual aids. Remember to keep within their realm of experience.

Little understanding of time and space

They live in the present and their concepts of time, space and distance are limited. Take care in using maps and dates, as they are often not appropriate. Simple maps, particularly 3-dimensional maps, and simple family trees can be helpful.

Gradually gaining independence

Don't treat them as babies; they want to be 'grown-up'. Give them opportunities to be creative and work independently. Perhaps you could give them jobs to do or somehow involve them in helping you. Remember that they still need clear guidelines for behaviour and close supervision because they are not always aware of the dangers and consequences of their behaviour.

Curious

They are full of questions about everything (e.g. how things work, or why things happen the way they do). Try to encourage this, because this is how they learn. However, some of their questions may be difficult to answer, so try to be prepared; think of questions that they may ask in a given lesson in order to be prepared for answering them.

Imaginative
They have great imaginations. Make the most of this in creative work.

Easily excited
Don't over-stimulate them. They can quite easily become over-excited and difficult to control. Aim to provide a calm atmosphere. All the same, harness their natural enthusiasm by doing activities that they enjoy.

Desire to please and be recognised by adults
They need and want adult approval. Encourage them as much as possible and respond positively to their work. Show love and care in your treatment of them. Allow them to help you by delegating small tasks to them. Be worthy of respect by being a godly model. Remember important events (e.g. birthdays) as this will mean a lot to them.

a. List three important characteristics of the age group of your class:

THINK AND PRAY

b. List three important things to remember when teaching them about God:

c. Pray for the children of your class by name, thanking God for how he has made them, and asking him to help you teach each one of them well.

Chapter 3

Teaching the Bible to children

In this chapter

1. General principles

a. Prepare well

If we are to teach children the Bible at all, then we need to teach it well. Teaching the Bible to children is often more difficult than it seems. It's tempting to take the attitude, "They're only kids", but this is a fatal mistake. The essence of good teaching to children is accurate simplification: that is, bringing the message of a Bible passage down to their level of understanding, without distorting it. This can't be done off the cuff. It requires much prayerful thought and preparation. It means working hard to understand a passage well, so that it can be simplified faithfully and you can be prepared to answer the many questions they are bound to ask.

b. Teach accurately and faithfully

Children aren't as discerning as adults; we need to take special care to teach the Bible accurately and faithfully to them. When simplifying a passage, we need to make sure that we don't change its basic meaning.

c. Teach prayerfully

Prayer is a very important part of preparation, since it is God who both enlightens us to understand his Word, and opens the hearts of the children to respond to it. We need God's help to teach God's Word to children.

d. Teach meaningfully

Children need to be taught what they are capable of understanding and so develop accurate concepts about God and the Bible. As we have seen already, what they are capable of understanding will vary from age group to age group, from class to class, and even among the individuals in your class. It's important to get to know not only the expected characteristics but the individuals in your care. Gradually you will learn what the children in your class are capable of understanding.

One of our main hopes as we teach children is that they will remember what we teach them. There is little value in teaching Bible passages that are beyond the children's comprehension, hoping that they will store the information and recall it when they are old enough to understand it. By the time they are old enough to understand it they will have forgotten it or have some vague confusing memory.

I might also add here that if you distort a Bible passage by adding to it rather than simplifying it, you may be surprised to find that the children remember your additions thinking that they come from the Bible. In later years when they realise that such details are not in the Bible, then they may look back with mistrust on the rest of your teaching as well.

Another thing that needs to be considered is the experience that the children in your class have had. We need to consider which elements of a Bible story will be unfamiliar to the children (e.g. don't assume that the children will know what a 'desert' or a 'well' is). Then think how these unfamiliar elements can best be explained to the children, using vocabulary that is familiar to them. We want the children to understand as much of the setting of a story as possible, so that they can focus their attention on the message we want them to learn.

e. Teach so children learn

When we teach children the Bible, it is not enough that we 'teach'—we want the children to 'learn'. And so we need to teach in such a way that the children learn.

For learning to take place, children need to hear, understand and remember the message you have taught. As a reminder to you, I have called this the HUR principle of learning. The children need to:

Hear
Understand
Remember

H is for Hear

Children aren't going to learn anything if they can't hear it. It's fundamental to speak loudly enough for children to hear you and to be conscious of any distractions (e.g. a high noise level from another class). Say the story at such a time in the lesson (i.e. not when they've already been sitting for a long time), and in such a way, that children can listen attentively.

U is for Understand

Children are prone to misunderstanding and confusion unless the meaning is clear. They do one of three things:

· they don't understand (it just goes over their heads);
· they misunderstand (it partly goes in but is not properly understood);
· they understand it (which is naturally what we want them to do).

We need to make sure that the children have understood what we have taught them in a given lesson. Thinking that the children will be able to understand is one thing; knowing that they have understood is another. What they understand you to be saying may not be what you intended to say. Therefore, questioning and revision are important.

R is for Remember

It is a challenge to consider how you can best help children remember the main message. Much of this book aims to stimulate your thinking on this. You want the message to be heard, the message to be understood and the message to be remembered.

Thoughtfully written action rhymes and songs are great assets in helping children remember things (more on this later). If children do take home an activity, make the most of the opportunity to use this in reminding them of what they've learnt (more on this in chapter 6).

a. Think back to the last few lessons that you have taught. How effectively have the children...
  heard the message?
  understood the message?
  remembered the message?

b. Which of the above areas do you need to work on?

c. What changes could you make?

d. How will you go about implementing these changes and ensuring that the children hear, understand and remember the message you are teaching?

e. Pray about these matters.

The following section is intended as a guide for teaching the Bible to each age group. It represents general principles which should be read as such, since children of a particular age group will differ greatly in their abilities to learn and understand the Bible. There are many factors which influence their ability to understand: for instance, whether the Bible is read at home, previous experience in Sunday School, Scripture lessons at school and their level of maturity.

2. Teaching two-year-olds about God

Few Sunday Schools have a class of two-year-olds. Usually two-year-olds are in creche, and Sunday School classes begin for pre-schoolers. However, wherever two-year-olds are, whether in a Sunday School hall or in creche, they can be learning foundational truths about God. It's a wonderful opportunity. I'm assuming that most time with two-year-olds will be in a creche set-up. Once they are two and a half going on three it might become more of a 'class', which I choose to call 'Transition creche', half-way between creche and Sunday School.

However, the following notes should be valuable for those involved with two-year-olds. Even in a creche set-up, a little bit of time can be spent with children gathering around a teacher and having a very simple story read to them. This, in fact, is an ideal way of teaching this age group.

a. What are two-year-olds learning?

Two-year-olds are busy learning about their world. They absorb much information and seem always ready to learn more. Their vocabulary is developing so that now they can ask questions about the world around them. Questions such as "What's this?" can form the basis of much of their conversation. At the same time, their conversational ability and vocabulary vary considerably—some are very vocal, while others (especially boys) may not talk much. They can usually understand far more than they can express. Occasionally, often when we least expect it, precious truths can be uttered, making us realise that they take in more than we think.

Learning about God the Creator should be a natural part of their learning about the world. Much can be learnt at home when children grow up from toddlerhood learning about God. Sunday School/creche can reinforce this and show them that God is a part of the lives of many people, not just their family. Sunday School/creche can also provide some direction and encouragement for parents in teaching their own children at home (e.g. by providing them with a copy of the syllabus).

b. What can we teach two-year-olds?

Essentially we want to teach them basic truths about God and his relationship with them, truths upon which they can build in later years as their understanding increases.

A fundamental place to begin is 'God made'. As they discover about the creation around them, whether it be in their own backyard or the zoo, they can be learning that God made the world around them.

Similarly, children can learn about themselves, realising that God made each part of them: fingers, toes, ears, eyes, face—in fact all of them. This can also be a way of learning to thank God ("Thank you God for my eyes so that I can see").

Another aspect of God that is helpful for a two-year-old to learn is God's love and care. Two-year-olds very much need love and security and acceptance. What precious truths to be able to share with our little ones: that God loves me, cares for me, and is with me.

Let's think for a moment what a two-year-old needs to know about their parents (assuming for the purposes of this illustration that they have loving parents): that their parents love them; care for them (give food etc.); enjoy being with them; help them in everyday tasks; that their parents are the boss. In a similar way, it's valuable for two-year-olds to learn about God's relationship with them—how God made us, loves us and helps us, how he's in charge, and so on.

c. Guidelines for teaching two year olds

- Learning about God needs to be focussed on their world, e.g. "God made my cat; God loves me; thank you God for my family". It is important to be specific, and to extend from specifics to generalities. Begin with their world ("God made this worm/leaf/flower") and then move on to generalities ("God made every worm/animal/thing"). Don't assume that two-year-olds will transfer the logic of a general statement.

- Teach one simple, basic statement at a time. For instance, "God made me" might be broken up into simple lessons like: God made my hands, God made my feet, God made my eyes and ears, and finally, God made all of me.

- Be repetitive. Young children like repetition. They like hearing the same stories and singing the same songs again and again. Short action rhymes and songs are a helpful means of learning.

- A valuable way to teach this age is to have a simple story on one page (it may only be about four sentences) with magazine pictures or simple drawings illustrating it. Slip the page into a plastic sleeve and then put it in a ring binder.

  Instead of trying to tell a formal story to a group of two-year-olds, you may find it easier to gather two children at a time and read the simple story while the other children play—this makes such a lesson workable in a creche situation. The reason I include the ring binder is that you can build it up over the weeks by keeping each story in the folder. Thus children can be looking over previous stories as well. Children of this age will very much enjoy looking through the folder, and this provides an ideal opportunity to revise previous lessons.

- Here's an example of a simple story. Point to different pictures as you tell the story:

  God made this tree.
  He made its trunk and branches and leaves.
  God made this tree too.
  He made tall trees and apple trees and gum trees—all kinds of trees.
  God made all the different trees.
  We can thank God for making all the trees.

- Remember that young children are very trusting. Much of their learning about the world is accepting what adults tell them. So be thoughtful and careful in your teaching.

3. Teaching the Bible to pre-schoolers (3-4 years)

Teaching the Bible to pre-schoolers is a little difficult to define. Some three-year-olds will really fit the description of two-year-olds, whereas the older four-year-olds can be much more advanced. Children grow so quickly in the early years that it is difficult to make generalised comments that apply to all pre-schoolers.

Therefore, it is important that you get to know what level of learning your children are capable of. Never over-estimate their learning abilities. It is far preferable to aim lower and ensure that all the children understand the story, than aim too high and have little comprehension as a result. You can always include more detail if they want to know more.

So let's see how you would move from preparing a story for two-year-olds to one for three- or four-year-olds.

Pre-schoolers enjoy books being read to them. They have a longer attention span than two-year-olds, so they can often sit still and listen for the duration of a simple picture book. They enjoy an actual story with a story line as opposed to the two-year-old picture book with captions. Pre-schoolers will enjoy greater detail in the story and like to hear about characters, particularly those with whom they can identify. So the thematic approach for two-year-olds can be partly replaced by character stories, like hearing about Old Testament characters and Jesus and his friends.

a. Where do we begin?

As with two-year-olds, an excellent place to begin with pre-schoolers is with God the Creator. Start with the God who made them and the world around them—and not just the little things, but the big things too, like the sun, the sky, the oceans and the mountains. Initially, there is some overlap with what I have suggested for two-year-olds, but many children begin Sunday School as a pre-schooler, and not before; and for those who have started earlier, it's valuable to go over these truths again. You still need to teach in specifics ("God made me… my family… my friends… and then… everyone"), and you will still need to carefully lead up to generalities (i.e. "God made everything" and "God made everyone").

Progress from God who made them (and the things around them) to God who loves them (and their families and friends) and to God who knows them. You are building a concept of God in their minds that encompasses both his greatness and his love. He's bigger than anything, and yet he loves us. God knows about the whole world and about each of us too.

Then move from God to God's book, the Bible—it's his special book, a true book, written a long time ago. Once we establish the Bible in this way, we introduce the children to Jesus, as the Bible tells us about Jesus—Jesus is God's son and he shows us what God is like, he can do things that we can't do.

You might wonder why I begin teaching pre-schoolers about God and then come to Jesus later. My reasons are that by beginning with God the children are learning about someone who is far different from themselves—Creator and sustainer, bigger than anything and someone we can't see. I have found that pre-schoolers can really catch onto the idea of how great God is and indeed who he is. Once they have a concept of God, then Jesus can be defined as God's Son, someone who shows us what God is like (Col 1:15,19). So Jesus is taught as so much more than just a man. If we begin with Jesus first, a pre-schooler with their concrete thinking will have trouble thinking of Jesus as more than a man. We want to teach them his divinity as well as his manhood, so we begin with God and then move to God's Son. Please note that I am in no way trying to belittle the importance of Jesus; rather I'm trying to preserve it by helping children see Jesus as being more than a man (Phil 2: 6-11).

It is beneficial for pre-schoolers to learn various aspects of knowing God which are relevant to their lives. For instance, it is valuable to teach the children truths about prayer (talking to God, thanking God, saying sorry) and about how God wants them to live (be kind, share, and so on).

b. Teaching Bible stories

Pre-schoolers can begin listening to Bible stories. Aim to move chronologically and slowly through the Old Testament only covering key characters like Abraham and David and spending a number of weeks on each so that the children have a chance to get to know that character. The Gospels provide us with much to learn about Jesus, including many stories that are very suitable for pre-schoolers.

Adults can have the attitude that we should be teaching as much of the Bible as possible in a year. Pre-schoolers need to go at a slower pace in order to learn. They need time to get to know biblical concepts and characters. And, importantly, they need to hear stories that can be understood. So never be anxious to cover too much of the Bible in one year.

As pre-schoolers don't have much of a concept of time and dates, it is best to spend a number of lessons on one time period. Rather than jumping from the Old Testament to the New Testament with a couple of weeks here and a couple of weeks there, a more systematic and chronological approach is preferable.

c. Stories with symbolism?

One reason why parts of the Bible are inappropriate for this age group is that pre-schoolers think concretely and are unable to think symbolically and abstractly. Thus our teaching needs to be concrete and literal.

Many of the parables of Jesus, for example, are inappropriate because pre-schoolers are not able to understand the symbolism. (In fact, as Mark 4 makes clear, Jesus' parables are in one sense designed to be difficult to understand.) Similarly, the 'I am' sayings of Jesus are inappropriate as they may be taken literally. If we refer to Jesus as a shepherd and say that we are his sheep, then a pre-schooler will take this literally. If you know that a story will be unhelpful for your class because they don't yet have the cognitive skills to understand it, then it is better to select a different story than to confuse them.

The problem is that we are often attracted to the very stories which are difficult for them to understand. Jesus as a shepherd or the bread of life may seem vivid to us, and suggest lots of ideas for good activities and visual aids. However, these are inappropriate stories for this age group. They simply will not make the symbolic connections, and will end up confused.

4. Teaching the Bible to infants children (5-7 years)

a. Now we are at school...

Infants' children are now at school and this has consequences for teaching them the Bible. Infants children are accustomed to being in a more formal learning environment. They are going through a period of rapid academic learning as they learn basic maths concepts, reading and writing.

Even so, we need to make sure that we don't over-estimate their growing mental capabilities. Knowing that they are learning to read and write, we can easily forget that their thinking skills are still quite immature. They still think at a concrete level and are capable of very little abstract reasoning and symbolism. We need to be literal in our teaching, our choice of stories and vocabulary.

b. Teaching infants children

Teaching the Bible to infants children can be a rewarding experience. They love to hear stories, particularly with action, and they have a greater ability to comprehend and remember stories compared with pre-schoolers. They are now old enough to cope with stories with more detail, and character studies can be in more depth. Much of the year's syllabus can be based on Bible passages. However, I would suggest that you still work through the Bible systematically without jumping around the Bible too much.

Infants children are able to understand about Jesus, his life and ministry in a way that they were previously too young to grasp. They are now able to put together all the parts of his life and not see them as isolated incidents. They can really begin to learn about the person of Jesus. Teach them about Jesus in such a way that they can respond to him and learn how to live as Jesus' follower. It is exciting being able to teach children about Jesus and seeing them learn to trust him.

c. Some things to remember

Infants children live in the present, and their concepts of time and space are poorly developed. This is not the age group with which to use time charts, dates and maps. Also, do not assume that children will be able to understand the chronology of the Bible. It is advisable to teach stories from the Old Testament and New Testament chronologically (e.g. 1 & 2 Samuel, followed by Kings).

Another consequence of this age group living in the present, is that the Bible stories need to be applied to their lives in the here and now. These children are keenly interested in the present, and not nearly as interested in the past or the future. Think through how the Bible can be applied to their lives when preparing the story. If all we seem to be doing from their eyes is giving them history lessons, then we will lose their interest and they won't see the relevance of the Bible for their lives. We want the children to see that the Bible is relevant to them and that God can be real to them.

In teaching the Bible we need to stress that it is reality and not fantasy. Children of this age group are learning to distinguish the fantasy world from the real world. It is often during these years that imaginary characters like the Easter bunny, the tooth fairy or Santa are exposed. We need to ensure that they do not consider the Bible as a book of fairy tales.

We should try to teach the children through all their senses. Children do not learn just through their ears. So visual aids are important, as are experiences that will bring other senses into the learning experience. Children of this age will learn the most if they are actively involved in learning—not just hearing and seeing but doing as well.

Finally, this age group needs security. They are going through years of change, from their home environment to school. Therefore, we need to teach about God in such a way that they see him as loving, unchanging, and faithful. If we teach God as a loving Father, we need some understanding of their family backgrounds. If you have children from single-parent families then you will need to think how God's fatherliness can be best explained (our Father in heaven as opposed to our fathers on earth). Be sensitive to the situations of your children. As I said before, we want to help them feel secure and loved by God.

▲ ● ■
THINK AND PRAY

a. Think of the age group that you teach.
What have you learnt about teaching God and the Bible to them?
List three important things that you have learnt:

b. Pray about the above and any changes that will need to be made to your teaching as a consequence.

Chapter 4

Step 1: Discover the message

In this chapter

So far we have looked at:

- what you should be like as a Sunday School teacher
- what children are like at their different ages and stages
- how, in general terms, you should teach them

Now it is time to get more specific. Over the next three chapters we will look at how to go about actually preparing a Sunday School lesson and delivering it. There are three basic steps, which I will outline in chapters 4, 5 and 6, with plenty of advice and ideas along the way.

First, just a word on the order of these steps. It is very common for Sunday School lessons to be 'driven' by the activity or visual aid. The teacher comes up with a great idea for getting the kids to construct their own fully functioning version of Elijah's altar on Mt Carmel, complete with simulated trench, water and fire from heaven. This idea then completely dominates the planning and presentation of the lesson for that Sunday. It may or may not have anything to do with what the episode is about in 1 Kings 18, or teach the children the important lessons which that Bible passage contains, but it nevertheless consumes most of the preparation and lesson time.

This is all the wrong way around. It is like hosting a dinner party, but spending the bulk of your preparation time folding the serviettes and selecting the background music, and then hurriedly heating up some baked beans at the last minute for the main course.

In preparing and presenting a Sunday School lesson, we must start with the Bible, and with the message that we want to communicate to the children for that week. The content of the message should shape and drive everything else we do. Only with the message clear in our minds, can we begin to plan the various activities that will make up the entire lesson.

(Note: throughout these chapters I will be using the word 'lesson' to describe the whole time you have your Sunday School class, the 'class time'. Some Sunday Schools have 'group times' at the beginning, where the children are all together for some singing and other activities. In that case, the 'lesson' would start when the children return to their individual classes.)

The three steps, then, in preparing a Sunday School lesson are:

1. Discover the message
2. Plan how to teach the message
3. Design the overall package

In this chapter, we will look at Step 1, and how we discover what message God wants us to convey to the children from the Bible.

Step 1a: Select

Please note: quite often you are given a syllabus to follow and have no choice as to which passages you are teaching. You may still find it useful to read this section and consider the passages you are to teach.

We have to be careful of how we use the Bible. There are two mistakes that can easily be made when choosing passages to teach. One is to choose a passage to support a particular theme or message, when the passage is not really about that theme. The other is to be so intent on teaching children the whole Bible that we teach passages which are beyond the ability of the children to understand.

So firstly, don't distort passages to fit a theme. And secondly, aim to teach passages that the children are capable of understanding.

It is easy to be attracted to a story because it has an appealing setting or characters, without considering its appropriateness in terms of what you would be teaching the children. Give careful thought before you gravitate towards stories with animals, boats or children, or some other face value appeal.

When you are selecting a Bible passage for a particular group of children, give thought to:
- what they are capable of understanding
- what they are capable of remembering
- what is meaningful to them

When deciding on a series of lessons or a term's syllabus, consider the following:
- Young children have little concept of time and dates—history is not their strong point!
- Therefore, as I have said previously, it is preferable to be chronological when teaching from the Old and New Testaments, i.e. Abraham before David and Jesus before Paul.
- Try to teach a series of lessons from one book of the Bible, thus aiming for consistency, rather than jumping around the Bible with a week here and a week there.
- If you are preparing a series of lessons on a topic rather than a book of the Bible, do so with care so that you are presenting a balanced, biblical coverage of the topic. Don't distort the Bible's picture of God to suit what you think is nice for children to know. For example, you may not wish to frighten young children with lurid stories of hell; but it is still quite appropriate (and very helpful) to introduce them to the concepts of sin and doing wrong, and of how God is angry when we do what is wrong.

Read the following passages and decide which would be suitable to teach three or four-year-olds, which would be suitable to teach five to seven-year-olds, and which would be unsuitable for both age groups. Give your reasons.

Genesis 12:1-9
Psalm 145:8-13
Mark 8:1-10
John 4:1-41
Romans 12:1-2
Hebrews 5:1-10

Step 1b: Understand

The most important preparation is the story, i.e. the verbal teaching component, which is usually a Bible passage, but may be a group of verses on a topic or doctrine. Teaching the Bible to children is really what Sunday School is all about. We need to treat the Bible with care and ensure that we set aside sufficient time in the week to read the passage properly and understand it. Then we are in a position to teach it.

a. Begin with the Bible

You may be working from story outlines in a manual, or you may be writing your own material. Either way, it is important that when you prepare a story you begin with the Bible. Remember that you are teaching the Bible and not a manual. If we read a manual or commentary first, then we have preconceived ideas of what the Bible is saying. If we read the Bible first, then we will have to think carefully about the meaning of the passage. This is advantageous because in our first reading we will probably have some questions about the passage. This will give us some idea of the sort of questions that our class might raise.

b. Reading the passage

i. When you read the passage, ask yourself the following questions:
    - What is the passage about?
    - Is the passage addressed to a particular situation or audience?
    - What are the main ideas or themes?
    - What don't I understand?
    - Are there any difficult words, phrases or concepts?
    - Are there any helpful cross-references?

ii. It is important that you are confident of your understanding of a passage. If you find that there are things that you do not understand, then make a note of them and refer to a commentary.

iii. To have really understood a passage, you must be able to isolate and state its main point or points—there may be more than one.

Regardless of the class you are teaching, what is the passage about? Concentrate on the passage and its meaning. Work out the main point of the passage before you start considering the age of your class and how you might communicate it.

A resource which may be helpful in knowing how to read and understand Bible passages is *Postcard from Palestine* by Andrew Reid (also published by Matthias Media).

To help you practise the different steps in preparing a lesson, I've included these 'Now you try' sections at a few places in chapters 4-6. In these exercises, you will go through all the steps necessary to prepare a lesson on Luke 8:22-25 (the story of Jesus calming the storm), from understanding the passage through to designing the whole package of the lesson. So that you can keep this material together and refer to it easily as you go along, we've put the whole exercise in Appendix A. Turn there now to page 182 and do 'Step 1b: Understand'.

▲ ● ■
NOW YOU TRY

Step 1c: Prepare

a. Main message

At this point, having worked hard on the Bible passage, you should be able to write a simple, brief statement of the main message you want the children to learn. In doing so, think about the age of your class and their level of understanding.

When writing the main message, be:
· specific
· brief
· simple

Now look at the manual if you are using one, and pay careful attention to the lesson aims and objectives. Hopefully they will be in agreement with what you discovered to be the main message from the Bible passage.

To give an example, in preparing a lesson on Luke 19:1-10 (the story of Zacchaeus), I came up with the following main message that I would attempt to convey to a pre-school class: *Jesus wanted to be friends with Zacchaeus and Zacchaeus changed when he became Jesus' friend.* (I'll keep using this Zacchaeus lesson as an example as we go along.)

b. Simplify the passage

The next step is a challenge. How can the passage be simplified so that my class will understand it?

- List any difficult vocabulary or concepts which are in the story and are important for the children to understand. Think of how you will explain them and/or simplify them. You need to remember the children's level of experience, and not assume that they will understand everything; e.g. words such as 'temple', 'disciple', and 'sin' will need either to be explained or replaced with another word which the children understand.

- Write a point form summary of the passage including all the important details you will need to tell the children.

- If you are using a manual or notes they should be of help in simplifying a passage. Often the passage will be simplified for you—but you need to make sure that the age group you are teaching will be able to understand the simplified version, as it may be aimed at older children. You also need to ensure that the simplified version is faithful to the Bible.

Another source of help is a children's Bible. There are many Bibles now available for children of all ages, from toddlers to independent readers. It might be worthwhile to buy a reputable children's Bible that is aimed at the age group you teach. There are also commentaries, Bible dictionaries, atlases and other reference books aimed at children. These may also be of help in understanding, simplifying and explaining a passage.

As an example, here is my simplification of Luke 19:1-10 aimed at pre-schoolers:

> Today we're going to hear about Jesus being friends with a man called Zacchaeus. People didn't like Zacchaeus. Zacchaeus had been mean and cheated people. He had lots of money and lots of things.
>
> Jesus was walking through the place where Zacchaeus was. Zacchaeus wanted to see Jesus but because he was short he couldn't see over all the people. So Zacchaeus ran to a tree and climbed it so that he could see Jesus.
>
> When Jesus came to the tree, he looked up and told Zacchaeus to come down because he was going to go to his house. Zacchaeus came down at once. Zacchaeus was very glad to meet Jesus.
>
> When Zacchaeus became Jesus' friend, he changed. He wasn't a mean man anymore. He wanted to give half of all his things to poor people. Zacchaeus wanted to be friends with Jesus and please him. He was happy that Jesus wanted to be his friend.

▲ ● ■

NOW YOU TRY

Go to Appendix A (page 183), and do Step 1c for Luke 8:22-25.

What's next?

Now you have a simplification of the passage and a main message that you want to reinforce. The next step is to think of how the passage can best be presented. What will be the most effective approach? A straight telling of the story, a puppet play, a drama? And what visual aids (if appropriate) can be used to help you tell it?

This is the content of Step 2: "Plan how to teach the message", in our next chapter.

Chapter 5

Step 2: Plan how to teach the message

In this chapter

You have your main message, and you have a simplification of the Bible passage from which that message was taken. How are you going to convey this content to your children?

Step 2a: Introduce

Children need to be motivated in order to listen and concentrate. If you have their interest *before* you begin the story, then you will find that you have their attention as well. This will make it easier to tell the story, and allow you to focus on the story rather than being distracted by the children's behaviour.

Before we look at specific ways to introduce a story, we need to think about what you want the children to remember. We have previously discussed the importance of isolating the main message you want to teach the children. We want to capture the children's attention in such a way that they hear the main message. So choose a form of introduction which focuses on the aim of the story, rather than on some insignificant detail.

So how do you gain their interest? How do you introduce a story so that they will be motivated to listen? Here are some ideas:

a. For 2 – 5 year olds
- Picture book or cards—you can show the children some pictures and ask them questions which will then relate to the story. For example, if you are teaching about how God made animals, you could show pictures of animals and talk about what each animal is like (their size, looks, sounds).
- Playdough or drawing—the children could be asked to make or draw something which then relates to the story (e.g. an animal). (Remember that their end products may bear little relation to what they are supposed to be!)
- Photos—young children enjoy looking at photos. If you are teaching that God made animals, you could show a photo of your pet (if you have one).
- Show an object and talk about it (e.g. a flower, seeds, shells).
- Action rhymes—these can be written fairly easily and so can focus on the main message (see chapter 6)
- Songs—a short song may be appropriate. You can then talk about the words of the song, which could lead into the story (see chapter 10 for information about songs).

b. For 5 – 7 year olds
- Show a portion of a picture and ask questions. What do you think is happening? Where do you think he is?
- The children can draw a picture related to the story.
- The teacher begins drawing a picture and the children guess what it is.

- Play hide and seek—the hidden objects are then used in telling the story. Alternatively, pictures could be hidden. Keep the children from getting too noisy with this activity.
- Play pass the parcel—objects or pictures are hidden in the parcel. Again be conscious of how excited the children become.
- A jigsaw—this could be combined with hide and seek or pass the parcel where the children could find pieces of the puzzle. The completed jigsaw could be a picture, verse or message.
- Preparation of visual aids—children can be involved in preparing the visual aid in some way (e.g. drawing and/or colouring a person; pasting cotton wool on a sheep outline)

c. An example

In my sample lesson on Zacchaeus (from chapter 4), here's how I introduced the story to my pre-school class:

I showed two puppets (dolls would have done) and said:

"This is Ben and this is Peter. They are friends. I know they are friends because they like playing together and… Oh, Ben wants to tell me something [he whispers in my ear]. Ben said that he wants to play with the blocks because he knows that Peter likes playing with blocks. Now Peter wants to tell me something [he whispers in my ear]. Peter said that Ben is a good friend because they like being together and playing together. Do you have friends like that? Do you have friends you like to be with?

"We're going to hear a story about a man becoming Jesus' friend. Let's see what happened after he became friends with Jesus."

Go to Appendix A (page 184) and work out an introduction for your lesson on Jesus calming the storm.

▲ ● ■
NOW YOU TRY

Step 2b: Tell

a. Learning the story

When you are telling the story to your children, it is far preferable to say it, rather than read it from a manual. In order to capture the children's attention and keep eye contact, you need to look at the children and not have your head buried in a book. This is particularly important for younger children. If you are to say the story, then you need to learn the key elements and this takes some preparation.

If you are using a manual with a story written in full, familiarize yourself with the story by reading it through a few times underlining the key phrases. If you do not have a manual, then I would suggest that you write a brief story outline in preparation (see chapter 4). Make use of spare moments (in the train or under the shower) to practise remembering and saying the story. You may also want to write brief notes that you can refer to when you tell the story to your class. These could even be written on the back of visual aids.

b. Reading a story

If you are not confident in your ability to remember and tell a story, then you could make a story book to be read to the class. This becomes a visual aid in itself. But remember, you need to be able to look at the children and not have your head down. So make a story book or story cards that are easy to hold in such a way that you can still look at the children (e.g. hold it out to one side and slightly forward). Write the text to be read on each page with a bold, colourful picture (this could be drawn or made with various collage materials).

c. Presentation tips

When telling the story to your class remember to be:

Visible and audible
· Children need to see and hear you.
· You need to see all the children.

Dramatic
· Command their attention.
· Hold their interest.
· Try not to feel self-conscious or embarrassed.
· Vary the volume and pitch of your voice.
· Use hand gestures or expressions where appropriate.

Visual
· Visual aids are valuable.
· Have something for the children to look at.
· See elsewhere in this chapter for ideas about visual aids.

Concrete
· Remember that the children think on a concrete level and not on an abstract level—this is why visual aids are important.
· Use the known to explain the unknown, i.e. refer to things that they are familiar with.

Aware of distractions
· Minimise distractions where possible, e.g. sit with your back to a corner or a wall so that when the children face you they only see a wall behind you, and not other classes.
· Don't let individuals within a class distract other children. It is important for all children to be able to listen to the story. Have fellow teachers on the look-out to stop children distracting each other while you are telling the story.

Observant

- Keep as much eye contact as possible as you tell the story.
- Don't become so preoccupied with what you are doing that you are unaware of what your children are doing (they may be losing concentration, staring into space, or distracting each other).

Simple

- Keep the ideas simple.
- Use simple language.
- Don't clutter the main facts of a story with too much detail.

Repetitive

- Emphasize the important points in the story.
- Repeat the main message you want to teach.

Short

- Don't expect children to concentrate for longer than is physically possible. Learn from experience how long you can expect your class to concentrate.
- Ensure that the children don't become bored

---

a. How can you seat your class so that they can see and hear you, and have minimal distractions?

▲ ● ■
THINK AND PRAY

b. Given your personality and gifts, how is it possible for you to be dramatic when telling the story?

c. List three things you could do to ensure that you are observant and develop eye contact.

d. Reading the Bible with infants children

A story doesn't have to be an exciting production every week. It is appropriate and helpful to read a story aloud straight from the Bible. A Bible that has a picture to go with the story can be helpful for kindergarten children. Many year 1 and 2 children are capable of listening to a story without an accompanying picture. And it is great for children to learn to listen to the Bible.

Here are some tips

· Make sure the version is suitable for your class.

· Select a story that is simple, not too long, and easy to listen to.

· Don't try this at the beginning of the year, but wait until you're confident that the children could sit and listen.

Reading the Bible to the children in this way has a number of advantages:

· The children know that it's a story from the Bible and not something you've made up.

· They can see that the Bible is readable.

· It makes the children more familiar with the Bible—breaking down the idea of it being a 'big book that just sits on a shelf'.

· It may encourage children to read the Bible at home.

Step 2c: Illustrate

Children learn through their eyes and not just their ears. In fact, they will often remember something that they have seen and heard far better than something they have simply heard. A visual aid, by definition, is something that can be seen and that aids story telling. Visual aids help to capture and hold children's interest and attention. They also help children to visualise the story.

Visual aids are important when teaching younger children. As children get older, the nature and use of visual aids will change. One reason for this is that a child's reading skills will eventually develop to an extent where they can read a Bible passage themselves, and some lessons will be the group reading together rather than the teacher telling the story. Another reason is that as children get older they will be looking at Bible passages which are not narrative and which are more appropriately studied than told.

When using visual aids ensure that your aids are appropriate to the story and help you tell it, rather than being a hindrance or distraction. Remember that visual aids are intended to be aids, and that the story should be central. If visual aids are visual then they need to be big enough to be seen and displayed, or used in such a way that all the children can see them.

Variety is important. Interest will soon be lost if you tell stories from week to week using the same type of aids. However, a short series of stories may use the same aids for consistency.

Children have a good imagination. This is a welcome relief for those of us who are artistically challenged! Don't use poor artistic skills as an excuse. Often the simpler the drawing, the better it is. Here are some ideas for visual aids.

a. Visual aids based on pictures

When using visual aids based on pictures:

- Ensure they are large enough to be seen by all the children.
- Colour them brightly—crayons, textas and paint are preferable to pencils.
- Keep pictures simple and clear for young children (so as to avoid distraction). Older children can appreciate more detail.
- Look at children's books for ideas of pictures which appeal to children.

What if you can't draw?

- Collect simple pictures from anywhere and everywhere which could give you ideas.
- Collect magazine pictures.
- Collect simple sketch drawings of faces and figures; e.g. from comic strips.
- Collect pictures from unexpected places; e.g. birthday cards, wrapping paper, calendars, advertising leaflets, brochures.
- Use collage instead of drawing; e.g. paste on facial features (round stickers for eyes, wool for hair, and so on).
- Use some of the outlines which we have included below. Mix and match!

Picture cards

My suggestion for a first-timer (or second or third-timer!) is this: have about four or five pictures to tell the story. Make your pictures large, simple and brightly coloured. Write a brief outline of the story on the back of the pictures. Hold the pictures in front of you, resting on your lap, so that as you tell the story you can have eye contact with the children and an occasional glance at your notes on the back. (This of course means that you must carefully decide the order in which you will hold and change your pictures, and which part of the story will be written on each card.) In this way the children have the pictures to focus on and you have the children in front of you to focus on.

Scrap book

Another variation on this idea is to have a scrap book with a simple story line written on each page beside colour pictures. The scrap book needs to be held in such a way that you can look at the children without having to turn your back to move pages.

Such a book could be used for a short series of stories so that at the end of the series you have a book which can be read in total as revision. This would suit a series of stories on a particular character—e.g. Abraham or David—which would become their life story.

Other picture based ideas

Blu-Tack pictures—add as you talk

Draw as you talk

Series of pictures

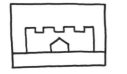
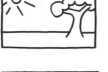

Board with opening windows revealing hidden pictures

Picture which opens

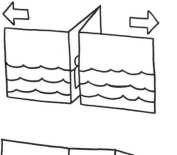

TV screen (made from a cardboard box)

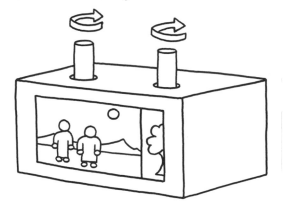

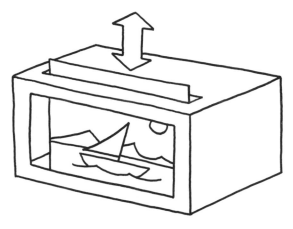

Concertina pictures

Sliding viewer

b. Three-dimensional models

Three-dimensional models are very effective. One idea is to use a piece of cardboard with a map or scene on it. Place it on the floor/table with the children seated around it. Free standing models (people out of cardboard rolls, buildings out of boxes or milk cartons) can be placed on it and moved as the story progresses

Another idea is to have a box on its side (inside decorated) and models standing inside the box (you may need to cut the top off so that the children can see inside clearly). This is particularly useful for a story which is set inside a house.

c. Story aprons

Here's an idea for someone who wants to try something new. A story apron is simply an apron, preferably with pockets. The teacher uses it to tell the story by pulling things out of the pockets or attaching things to the apron. For example, for 'Jesus feeding the 5000' you could have some cardboard fish and bread in your pocket and then a picture of all the baskets of food left over. It's easy to keep eye contact with the children as you are wearing the visual aid.

A story apron can be used more than once because the children will enjoy wondering how you will use it each time. Are you hiding something in the pockets? Will a puppet appear from behind its folds?

Where can I get one, you ask? You can often pick up cheap cloth aprons at a bargain shop; even a peg apron will serve the purpose. A male teacher may prefer a BBQ apron. If you (or a skilful friend) want to make an apron, it needs to be made from plain fabric. Here's a diagram with ideas:

d. Puppets

Puppets add a completely different dimension to your storytelling, and provide an ideal opportunity for maximum eye contact between the teacher and the class. Puppets will test the use of your voice and challenge you to vary your pitch, tone and volume. Other advantages of puppets are that they can effectively be made by the non-artistic, and children will relate well to them.

There are many different ways in which puppets can be used. Here are some ideas:

i. For the first timer
Use a story with two main characters. Make your puppets from cardboard rolls: draw or paste on a face, wrap around paper or fabric for clothes, and glue on wool or cotton wool for hair. Do not cover the lower opening. When using the puppets, place two fingers inside them and move them up and down as you speak. If a puppet is not in a particular scene then either put your hand behind your back or lay the puppet on your lap.

ii. If you teach by yourself

- You could use puppets for a story which has two or three main characters (i.e. one puppet in each hand and one on your lap). Choose puppets that are easy to hold; e.g. on sticks, glove puppets, or made from cardboard rolls.
- You could have just one puppet and interact with it. The story could be told through the puppet. Alternatively, the puppet could be one of the characters from a story and you could question it.
- You could have a combination of picture cards and puppets. This would suit a story where there are more than two characters and which takes place in a few different settings. Make the puppets out of cardboard and glue fabric on the front as clothes. Have a few large background cards with pictures of each setting. Rest the first picture card on your lap and move the characters across the picture as appropriate. When a character stays in one place, stick them on the picture with Blu Tack (which has been put on them previously). When one scene is over, then put that card down and pick up the next one. This method of storytelling is for the experienced teacher rather than the first timer.

iii. If you teach with one or more other teachers
- One teacher can be the narrator and other teachers can move the puppets.
- Each teacher can hold a different puppet and act out the story (with each teacher saying the lines for their puppet).

iv. If you are willing and ready to use puppets

Here are some ideas of what to use to make them. Puppets can be made out of:

- socks
- stockings stuffed with a soft stuffing
- newspaper rolls
- cardboard rolls
- paddle-pop sticks
- wooden pegs
- felt hand puppets
- paper plates
- boxes (e.g. match boxes, milk cartons)
- bottles (e.g. PET bottles, cordial bottles)
- wooden spoons
- kitchen implements (e.g. whisks)
- paint brushes (bristles as hair)
- paper bags
- tennis racquets

Pipe cleaner arms

e. Alternatives to visual aids

i. Child involvement

Try to involve the children in any way that is appropriate—holding, moving and adding objects, doing actions, making noises, and so on. Interaction by the children will help interest, concentration, memory and behaviour. Just ensure that children don't become silly and so detract from the story. You need to be in control and give clear guidelines as to what you want the children to do.

ii. Drama

In drama, the children are actively involved in the story, but it needs to be well managed in order to be effective. Younger children could be involved in a dramatic presentation of a story by simply wearing one article of clothing (e.g. a shawl or hat), and doing one action when you direct them (e.g. shake their hands, wave, clap). This allows controlled involvement that is appropriate for their age. You can be more adventurous with older children provided that you know them well and feel that it would work. Drama is particularly useful if you are telling a familiar story. Children who may otherwise have been bored can be actively involved.

iii. Reading a passage

See point d on page 56.

f. For new teachers

A new teacher needs to develop confidence in storytelling. At this stage, technique is more important than imaginative visual aids. Eye contact is one of the key things to learn. You also need to develop skills in varying the pitch and volume of your voice. Confidence in talking to a group of children takes time to develop.

With these things in mind, I would suggest that the first type of visual aids to use are picture cards. You could then move on to a scrap book, which is similar to picture cards and yet sufficiently different to be a change.

When you have the confidence to try something new and quite different, then I would suggest that you use puppets. Try not to be too ambitious! If you have a suitable story with two main characters then have a go. Puppets will give you experience in developing confidence in speaking to a class.

g. For more experienced teachers

Try to be more adventurous and creative. If you think of a unique visual aid that works well, it will stick in the children's memory longer than otherwise. An interesting variety of visual aids also helps with the management of the children. They will be more attentive and better behaved if you have captured their interest with something new and interesting. Bored children will remember little, act inappropriately and be a distraction to others.

A more imaginative use of puppets and three-dimensional models will extend your teaching skills and give added interest to your stories. Drama and child involvement are well worth trying. The first time you use such methods will probably involve considerable time in preparation, but this should diminish with experience. Don't give up too quickly!

h. An example

For my story on Zacchaeus, I came up with two ideas for illustrating the story to a pre-school class—the first fairly simple (ideal for new teachers), the second a little more demanding (but probably more effective):

i.   A straightforward way to illustrate this story is to prepare picture cards. Five or six simple drawings could be photocopied and brightly coloured. Paste these into a scrap book or onto card to use when telling the story.

ii. A more complex but probably more effective idea is to make a puppet for Jesus and Zacchaeus. Then attach a felt tree to an apron or tee-shirt and use this as the 'scenery' for Jesus and Zacchaeus to act out the story. Alternatively you could draw a tree on a sheet of butchers' paper and pin it to your top. Jesus can walk towards the tree and Zacchaeus can be in it.

▲ ● ■
NOW YOU TRY
Turn to Appendix A (page 184) and have a go at preparing a visual aid for your developing lesson on Luke 8:22-25.

Step 2d: Conclude

We've just told the story and it went well. We prepared an effective visual aid. We learnt the story well. The children seemed to be interested and involved. But what now? How do we finish it and move onto the next part of the lesson? It is easy to find ourselves sitting with a blank look, thinking about what to do or say.

You need to have the main message of the story firmly in your mind so that you can reinforce it after the story has been told.

a. Ideas for concluding the story

·   State the main message; e.g. "So wasn't it great to hear that…"
·   Use the visual aid to conclude the story; e.g. if you have used concertina pictures to tell the story, open them out and see if the children can tell you what is happening in each picture.
·   Ask questions about the story, and in particular, the main message of the story (see below on Questioning).
·   If you have a puppet who has been 'listening' to the story, it might

whisper some questions or comments in your ear for you to repeat to the children.

- Pray as soon as you have finished the story; e.g. thanking God for what was heard, praying in response to what was heard, or praying for each other in the light of what was heard.
- Explaining the activity as soon as you have finished the story is a way of reinforcing the main message and reminding them of what the story was about; e.g. "We have just heard… and now we are going to make… so we can remember that…". If you have the main message written on the activity then read it to the children so they know what it says and how it relates to what they have just heard.
- A memory verse taken from the passage is a great way of concluding a story. It's an ideal way of reinforcing the fact that what they have just heard does come from the Bible, and here's a bit of it for them to remember (see the section on Memory Verses in chapter 6).
- For younger children, an action rhyme or a song can conclude a story, reminding them of the important truths from it (see the section in chapter 6 on Action Rhymes and the section in chapter 10 on Singing).

In whatever way you choose to conclude the story, ensure that you have something prepared to say or do, while the story is still fresh in everyone's mind. God wants us to remember what we learn from the Bible and to take it seriously (see James 1:22-26). If we show the children that the story is the key part of the Sunday School lesson, and that everything else relates to it, then we are conveying the importance of the Bible and what it says. If the story seems to be an isolated 'thing we do at Sunday School before we get on and do the fun stuff' then we are creating an unhelpful impression. So try and make the story central and build the lesson around it, so that the children can see its importance.

b. Application to their lives

When we teach the Bible to children, it is vital that we apply it to their lives. As adults we often automatically make the step of applying what we read to our lives, almost without realising it. Children do not make this step in application automatically. We need to show the relevance of what we're teaching to their own lives.

There may be some passages that don't have 'life applications' as such, but are teaching important truths about God. Don't regard such passages as not being relevant to children. We want children to learn about God's character so that they can grow in their understanding of, and faith in, God.

There may be other passages that talk about men and women who are examples to us of faith and godly living. Or, conversely, may be warnings to us of the consequences of ungodly living. Applications from such passages need to be done with care. We are not trying to make our children into mini-versions of Abraham, Moses or David.

But we can help our children to learn from their example and be encouraged by God's care and protection of them. I have found Graeme Goldsworthy's book *Gospel and Kingdom* to be very helpful in this whole area, especially in relation to applying Old Testament stories.

c. Questioning

When we want to revise a lesson, recall last week's lesson, conclude a story or discuss a topic with children, we will find ourselves asking children questions. Questioning children is a valuable way of finding out what they have understood, what they have remembered and what their thoughts and opinions are. Questioning children is an art that develops with practice.

i. Wording a Question

What words should we use to begin a question? The best words are: who, how, what, where, when and why. All these words require a child to think of an answer rather than simply say yes or no. A question calling for a yes/no answer is a closed question. It doesn't lead to discussion. You could say that they are dead-end questions.

On the other hand, questions beginning with who, how, what, where, when or why cannot be answered with just a yes or no. Many questions that are yes/no questions can be reworded so that the children have to think of an answer.

Here are some examples:

- "Was David's son called Solomon?" (closed) can be reworded as "Who was David's son?"
- "Did the Israelites spend forty years in the desert?" (closed) can be reworded as "Where did the Israelites go? For how long?"
- "Was Hannah happy?" (closed) could be reworded as "How did Hannah feel?"
- "Did Paul go to prison?" (closed) could be reworded as "When did Paul go to prison?"
- "Was Paul arrested for preaching?" (closed) could be reworded as "Why was Paul arrested?"

Another way of changing closed questions so that children have to think of answers, is to add "Why?" after a yes/no question. So using an example from above: "Was Hannah happy?" could be followed by "Why?". Using the word 'why' in a question is helpful because it can't be a one word answer.

If we are using questions as revision or to conclude a story, it might be worthwhile to write a few questions beforehand. That way you will know exactly what to say and will not be fumbling around for words, or find yourself asking only closed questions.

ii. When no-one answers

What do you do if you have asked a question and no-one answers? Firstly, try to reword the question and the children might have a better understanding of what you are asking. If there is still no answer, another teacher may be able to step in and say the answer. Alternatively, you could answer your own question, beginning with, "I think.." and then finishing with, "Is that right?". Hopefully they will at least be able to say "yes" (or nod their heads).

If the reason that the children didn't answer your question was that they didn't know or couldn't remember the answer, you may need to revise the lesson. Your question was actually successful in revealing the fact that the children need further explanation or revision in order to understand and remember.

However, children may not answer a question simply because they are shy or feel uneasy. If you have a class full of shy children who tend to be speechless when you ask questions, you may need to ask just one question that you are prepared to answer and leave it at that till next week. Gradually they may develop confidence, but don't push them. A great way of doing revision in a question/answer style which is not intimidating for shy children is to have a puppet which 'listens' to the story. At the end of the story you can ask the puppet questions, it answers in a 'whisper' in your ear and then you tell the class and 'check that the puppet was listening well'. Another way of questioning shy children is to do so while they are doing the activity after the story—that way they are not 'in the spotlight'.

iii. When answers are incorrect

You will find that answers are not always correct. It is often difficult to know how to deal with an incorrect answer. If the correct answer is important, then you may have to respond to the child with a polite and loving correction. Children need to be told when their understanding is in error. However, there are encouraging and discouraging ways of reacting, so watch your words!

Sometimes, a child might give an answer that is not what you were thinking of, but is not wrong in itself. If that is the case, don't react with a negative reply. Rather, admit that you had not thought of that answer. You may even find yourself learning from your children's viewpoint. You can then ask for other possible answers.

d. An example

For my story on Zacchaeus, delivered to a pre-school class, I worked out this simple conclusion:

> So wasn't it great that Jesus wanted to be Zacchaeus' friend? Remember, people didn't like Zacchaeus, but Jesus did want to be Zacchaeus' friend. And when Zacchaeus became Jesus' friend, he was very glad and he changed.

Turn to Appendix A (page 184) and work out how you will conclude your story.

NOW YOU TRY

Chapter 6

Step 3: Design the overall package

In this chapter

There is more in a lesson than the story. The other components of the lesson can be valuable in reinforcing the main message, and can assist the children in understanding and remembering it. The main message should dictate the content of the lesson and be repeated a number of times in the lesson. So what will you decide to do in the rest of the lesson? How will you design an overall package, so that each component reinforces the main message? For example, how will you utilise activities or craft (such that the message can be taken home)? What about the place of prayer, songs, action rhymes, quizzes and memory verses?

Let's look at the various components that can surround and reinforce the story, and that together make up the overall package of your lesson.

Step 3a: Select other components

a. The activity

What the children take home is a statement of what the lesson was about. This is a valuable learning/reinforcement tool both for the children and the parents. Make the most of this opportunity by ensuring that the children have something to take home which has a clear, simple message encapsulating what you want them to remember. Include Bible references where possible and appropriate. This has the advantage of telling Christian parents what the children have learnt and what they can talk about with them. It also means that non-Christian parents can be learning what Christians believe and what the Bible says.

The activity is also fun! Make the most of this opportunity to have fun with the children and do enjoyable activities—another way of helping them to want to come to Sunday School. School-age children usually enjoy craft, and don't have as many opportunities to do it now they are at school.

The following pages have lots of craft ideas to get your imagination going. The challenge, if you give children a craft activity, is to think how a message can be included on it or added to it.

Please remember that the children don't have to do just one activity. It's great to have a combination—maybe a word-based sheet/activity and then a more craft-like activity.

If you are using a manual with set activity sheets for each lesson, please give thought to the fact that the constant use of activity sheets can become regimental for the teachers and boring for the children. You are not obliged to use the activity sheets every week just because they are there. Children need variety; their interest needs to be captured and enthusiasm sparked. In planning a term, give careful thought to which activity sheets would be suitable to use. Then decide whether you want them to feature as the main activity for a given lesson or whether they will be done after another activity is completed. If you vary their use in this way, then you will actually be making them more useful. When deciding on which activity sheets to use and when, look at them from both the teacher's and the child's point of view. Does the activity sheet say what you want it to say? Is it reinforcing the main message you want to teach and you want the children to remember? Would it be interesting and enjoyable for the children to do? Would it be too difficult or too easy for the children in your class?

Preparing and presenting the activity

It's very easy to spend time finding a suitable activity and forgetting to think about how it will be done in the lesson. Any given activity can be done in a variety of ways, and it is up to you as the teacher to decide beforehand exactly what you want the children to do and how you want them to do it.

Let's look at how an activity can be prepared and presented using a specific example—making people.

- **The task**

Think through exactly what you want the children to do. Consider the time limitations and the length of time it will take the children to complete the task.

The children could:
- paste the outline of a person which has been pre-cut
- draw the features
- colour the clothes
- paste on the clothes (pre-cut)

When considering which of the above you want the children to do, think of their abilities, the time available, and their concentration spans.

- **Preparation**

Think of your limitations during the lesson. Do as much as possible before the lesson so that there aren't long delays while children have to wait for you.

You will not be able to cut out five figures at once during the lesson. Nor will you be able to write a verse/message on each one at the same time.

- **Organization**

Think of what you want where. Be organised. Don't be scratching around for what you need.

Let's say the figures are pre-cut, but you want the children to tear and paste crepe paper for clothes and draw on the features. Ensure that you have paste jars, pencils or textas, squares of tissue paper, and pre-cut figures all laid out on a shelf or table ready to be placed on the working table when required.

- **Instructions**

Think through the instructions that you will give the children. How will you explain the activity so that they understand what to do? Also consider where you want the children to be sitting to ensure that they have your attention.

It is usually best to explain the activity directly after the story. This is not only when you already have their attention, but it enables you to explain the relevance of the activity to the story (e.g. "We're now going to make...so we can remember that...").

Explain the activity step by step (e.g. "First you'll put some glue on... then you will paste squares of paper like this and...").

- **Completing the activity**

It is wise to put on the table only what is required for each step as it is being completed. This allows you to keep control, and means that you are able to give the children more direction with less opportunity for them to get carried away on their own unique creations.

Always do the activity in an orderly fashion. Have all the children doing one thing at a time with only those materials needed on the table. Then take those materials away before proceeding to the next step. You will probably need to repeat your instructions for each step of the activity as they are doing it.

Once the children have finished, put their work on a table away from the work area so that they are preserved from tampering hands.

Catering for the fast and slow

Children vary in the time it takes them to complete a task. As you get to know the children in your class, one of the things to observe is their approach to written work and craft activities. Some children will be conscientious and particular, taking time to complete a task accurately and carefully. Other children will have a more slap-dash approach. They may be more task-oriented; more concerned about finishing an activity rather than giving attention to the quality.

Here are some suggestions for handling the fast and slow:
- If you are giving the children more than one activity, just give them what you want them to take home first (i.e. what you want them to complete in the lesson).
- Give clear directions as to what you want the children to do, and ensure that they have understood.
- Special directions may need to be given to individual children. As you get to know them, you will know whether a child needs to be told more specific instructions than other children.
- Always have back-up activities to give the children if they finish early; e.g. a picture they could draw, writing out the main message or memory verse, or telling a teacher the story. Never tell children

to sit and wait until everyone has finished as this will lead to boredom and misbehaviour.

- Activity sheets can be useful to give children when they complete a craft activity. They can easily be finished at home if not finished in the lesson.
- Children who complete their work before others may be able to help you in some way.

Individual or group work?

For reasons stated earlier, I would encourage you to have something that the children can take home each week; that is, some individual reminder of the main message of the story. However, this may not necessarily be the primary activity that the children do. For five- to seven-year-olds, it may be a quick individual activity that is then followed by group work.

Young children aged 2-4 years are not really capable of successful group work. Two-year-olds tend to do things alongside each other, rather than together. Pre-schoolers are learning about group work but still may not be entirely ready. Doing a mural together may be quite a feat to organize. They are also very proud of their work and like to have it to keep.

Infants children are becoming more capable of group work, largely through experiences at school. They still like to take their work home, however, so it would be ideal to do a combination of individual and group work. They would be capable of leaving work at Sunday School to add to and take home the following week; e.g. a book which is progressively added to.

Murals and collages would be suitable activities for group work. Also the children could draw individual pictures, which are collected and pasted together to make a mural.

Activity ideas for two- to five-year-olds

- **The scribble sketch**

This age group cannot do precise or artistic colouring or drawing, but they enjoy the activity of scribbling. Don't get upset if their attempt to 'colour something in' results in a messy, unattractive outcome or if it ends up all one colour. Their main focus in doing such an activity is the process rather than the end product. Giving them an opportunity to make a contribution to an activity by scribbling gives them a feeling that it is theirs.

Some children will proudly show it to Mum and Dad, while others won't be all that interested. Parents will be pleased with the end product regardless of what it looks like—they like to see their children doing activities, and don't want to see a beautiful work of art which has obviously been done by the teacher.

- **Tricks with glue-sticks**

I define pasting as putting paper where glue has been spread by the teacher (i.e. plonking paper on paste). Two-year-olds love playing with glue-sticks and glue pots, and in their hands you may find glue ending up all over the paper, table, clothes, floor and many other places.

When pasting is required, it is wise to have the teachers use the glue sticks and put the glue where they want it. Then all the children have to do is place whatever is being pasted onto the glue. That way you will be able to control the end product, and a tree will end up with brown paper on the trunk and not in the clouds!

If you are intending that they paste two different colours in two different places, it is important that you offer the children only one coloured paper at a time. For example, if the children are pasting green paper squares as leaves in a tree and brown paper squares as bark, then only offer them green paper to begin with and only put glue on the branches. Then take the green paper away and only offer them brown paper and only put glue on the trunk. The end result is a tree!

Older pre-school children are capable of using glue-sticks themselves with close teacher direction. Glue-sticks are manageable for little hands and tend to be less messy than glue pots. The disadvantage is that they are more expensive. So, if glue pots are all that you can use, extra care is needed with supervision.

- **Words of warning**

Ensure that each child's name is on their work (either write names on the activity soon after the children begin or have names on stickers which you can quickly pull off and place on their work).

Occasionally a child may rip up what they do before it gets to the parents. This is usually for the enjoyment of the ripping process rather than because they didn't like what they did. So try to keep completed work out of reach till the parents come.

A great idea is to have a cloth, or wipes, handy to wipe messy fingers!

Always be mindful of safety during the activity time. Keep all scissors and staplers out of the children's reach. When using split pins, stick masking tape over the top of the split pin to avoid injury from the sharp ends. Also, if you use coat hangers for mobiles, put masking tape over the ends of the wire.

- **Drawing and colouring ideas**
- Make a stapled booklet—children are given a few sheets of paper, one at a time, each with a different picture and a text printed at the bottom of the page. Each page may require colouring, drawing, or even pasting. Due to their age, they will not take long to complete each page. When one page is finished, put it aside in a safe spot while the next page is done. Once the children have completed each page, they are assembled by a teacher and stapled. A title page can be added. The advantage of this activity is that the children can read the booklet through the week and be reminded of the story. You

might question why I am suggesting a booklet rather than a single page. The answer—they work so quickly (and lose quite quickly), and a booklet will not take them long.

Whenever you make booklets as an activity, give the children only one page at a time with clear instructions as to what they are to do. Collect the first page before handing out the second page. An easy way of collating the booklets is to put the first page (once completed) for each child's booklet face down on a table and add each page as they are completed. Then the pages can easily be stapled together.

- Make a folded book—use an A4 sheet of paper and fold horizontally and then vertically to make a book (see diagram on page 80). If pictures are drawn on the page and then photocopied for the children to fill in (by colouring or pasting), follow the page layout on the diagram so that the pictures end up facing the right way up.
- Make a scroll—a long picture or series of pictures could be drawn or coloured (again with a text underneath). It could then be glued onto cardboard rolls and thus becomes a scroll.
- Assemble a milk carton picture or mobile—divide a sheet of paper into four sections (each being the size of one side of a milk carton). The children draw or colour a series of pictures that tell the story. Once completed, glue the paper around a milk carton and attach a string so that it can be hung. For very young children, a cream carton could be used with some pasta or a bell inside, and it can become a shaker (ensure that it is adequately glued).
- Make a circular picture—divide a circle into three of four segments. Draw or colour a picture on each. Once completed attach another circle (with one segment missing) over the top with a split pin. The second circle can be revolved to reveal the pictures.

- **Pasting Ideas**

How do you incorporate the use of paste, without it being the same activity each week? Here are some ideas:

Variations on pasting paper:
- tear and paste
- paste cut-out pieces
- roll up crepe paper squares and paste
- tightly rolled tissue paper in different colours
- scrunched-up crepe paper, tissue paper or cellophane
- small mosaic pieces of coloured paper

Other collage material which can be pasted:
- cellophane
- cotton wool balls
- corrugated cardboard
- fabric

- orange bag netting
- foil
- old greeting cards
- leaves
- ribbon scraps
- wrapping paper
- wool scraps
- poly packing
- streamers
- magazine pictures
- macaroni (strong glue)

For sticking without glue:
- pre-cut and pre-glued stamps and coloured shapes (moisture to be added)
- round coloured stickers
- contact paper (can be cut into shapes before backing is peeled off)
- 'home-made' stickers, using computer address labels that children scribble on to add colour

Things (other than paper) to paste onto:
- tissue boxes—decorate the box and/or put something inside with a caption on the box or on the enclosed item.
- shoe boxes—can be used to make a bed or a room for a person (made from cardboard or a cardboard roll)
- paper plates—see page 82
- milk cartons—see page 86
- cardboard rolls—see page 83
- paper bags—see page 85

- **Threading ideas**

Older pre-school children enjoy threading. If they are threading onto string, you will need to attach a length of plastic straw to the end (with masking tape) so that the children can use this as a 'needle' to thread with. Whatever they are threading, a cardboard shape with a message from the lesson can be included. Make sure that you knot something at the end of the string so that their hard work doesn't slide off!

Things to thread:
- macaroni
- foil
- cut up straws
- halved cardboard rolls
- plastic beads
- cotton reels
- egg carton humps

- small, coloured cardboard strips stapled to make rings
- cardboard shapes (with holes punched in them)
- plastic lids (small, with drilled holes)

Activity ideas for five- to seven-year-olds
- **Suitable activities include:**
- drawing
- colouring in (can use crayons, pencils or textas)
- pasting
- stickers (e.g. round stickers or star stickers)

I would not advocate children using scissors. Many children are unable to use them proficiently and they can be dangerous even in the hands of those who can use them. I know of one child who cut himself with a pair of 'children's safety scissors' and needed medical attention. Where things need to be cut out, I see this as part of the teacher's preparation.

Take care if you choose to use paints. They require a fair amount of setting up, cleaning up and special equipment, as well as being messy for children's clothes. If you would like to use them, I suggest that you wait until you get to know your class and how easy it will be to paint in an orderly manner. Think about how best you can avoid getting paint on the children's clothes. This is much less of a problem if you use water-based paints.

Ensure that each child's name is on their work (either write names on the activity soon after the children begin or have names on stickers).

- **Craft Activities**

Some craft activities can be related to the story and can incorporate a message on them. Here are some ideas:
- puppets—a character from a story could be made from a cardboard roll, milk carton, plastic bottle or paper bag. A caption could be attached to them.
- modelling—we tend to think of younger children when we think of modelling, yet older children enjoy it too. People or items from a story could be made and/or small scenes can be assembled on a foam tray with a caption attached. Children can work with play-dough or plasticine.
- mobiles—can be made from any number of things. They can be abstract (using junk materials, foil, cellophane, etc.) or represent characters and items from a story.
- "the junk session"—bring in lots of boxes, containers of various shapes and sizes, old wrapping paper, scrap material, wool, string and other pieces of junk. The children create a specified object from a story.
- television sets—make them from boxes. The children draw or colour pictures to slot inside or go on a roll.

- **Short activity followed by craft**

Another good idea is to give the children a short activity that contains a reminder of the lesson (it might be word-based, like an activity sheet) and then follow it with a longer time spent on a craft activity.

The short activity based on the lesson may take the form of:
- a coded message which has to be decoded
- a message written in reverse which needs a mirror to read correctly
- a jigsaw puzzle which has a picture one side and a verse on the back (and can be pasted together when completed)
- a simple crossword puzzle
- filling out a memory verse

- **Written work**

Instead of having printed activity sheets each week, here are some alternative ideas:
- a reverse crossword puzzle—the children write the clues for a completed crossword. This could become a game where the children work in pairs, each pair with a different crossword. They write their clues on a second sheet of paper with a blank crossword, then swap and try to complete each other's crossword. N.B. it needs to be very, very simple.
- a book—children can make a book, which is added to each week during a series of lessons. The advantage of this activity is that they have something to read afterwards. The book would probably have to stay at Sunday School until it has been completed.
- comic strip—children draw pictures to go with given captions
- find a word—children have to hunt for selected words which are relevant to the story.
- a booklet—a page can be folded as illustrated below to make a simple booklet.

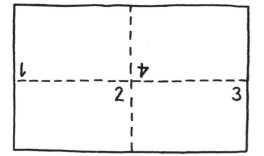 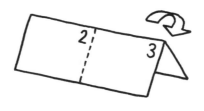 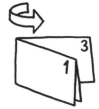

- **Preparation for the story**

Some activities are suitable to do before the story, in preparation for it. If the children are involved in helping to make the visual aids for a story, then they will be all the more motivated to listen. Here are some ideas:

- overhead projector transparencies—if you have access to an overhead projector, you could give each child a transparency and a scene to draw. You could then tell the story using their drawings.
- puppets—simple puppets can be made as characters in the story from cardboard rolls, paper plates or paper bags.
- a scene—if you get a large piece of heavy cardboard it can form the basis of a scene. Children could paste on paper and other collage materials to make a river, desert, street or whatever is in the story. If you have a large class, other children could make the characters for the story out of cardboard rolls, which will then be able to stand up on the scene.
- pictures to slot into a TV screen—children can each draw a picture depicting a different scene in the story (the teacher gives a brief description of the contents of each picture to each child). These pictures are then slotted into a TV screen made from a cardboard box (see description in chapter 5 on visual aids) and used to tell the story.

An example

For my story on Zacchaeus, the activity I selected was for the children to make a Zacchaeus puppet (similar to the one I had used in telling the story). I used a cardboard roll for the puppet, with scraps of fabric or wrapping paper for clothes, and wool or brown paper for hair. I wrote on the back of each puppet: "Jesus was Zacchaeus' friend".

Look back over the activity ideas above. Think about the message you are wanting to reinforce in your sample lesson (about Jesus calming the storm). Now turn to Appendix A (page 185) and write down an activity you would do with your chosen age group.

NOW YOU TRY

Craft ideas: *what to make with a paper plate*

Bag

A paper plate cut in half and stapled together with a handle stappled on.

Boat

A paper plate cut in half and stapled together with a straw mast and paper sails.

Fish

Paste on fins and tail. An adult will need to cut out the mouth.

Plate!

Paste on fruit cut-outs or rolled up crepe paper squares.

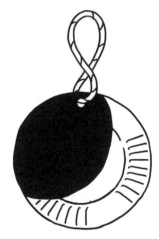

Sun/Moon mobile

Draw the moon on one side (you could paste on black paper for the sky). Paste yellow paper scraps on the other side for the sun.

Puppet

Attach a cardboard strip to the back and paste on facial features and clothes.

Spider or crab

Add flexi-straw segments as legs.

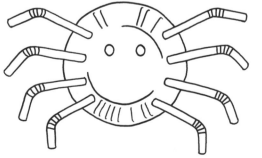

Mask

Paste on brown paper scraps as the mane and paste or draw facial features.

Craft ideas: *what to do with a cardboard roll*

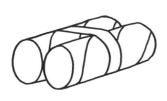

Binoculars
"To see God's world".

Candle
A pipe cleaner wick with a tinsel or paper flame.

Cradle
Cut in half length wise and add a baby.

Shaker
Put a small amount of rice inside. Cover both ends well with thick paper and tape. Decorate with stickers.

Mobile
An adult will need to punch holes in the top of the rolls for string. Some rolls could have a message on them.

Necklace
An adult will need to cut the rolls for children to decorate by pasting on paper and/or words.

Prop up puppets
To prop up puppets or pictures for a 3D display attach a cardboard roll to the back.

Horse
An adult will need to make slits to insert head and tail, and holes to insert pipe cleaner legs.

Puppet
Puppet person fits on fingers or stands. Wrap around paper clothes.

Tree
Make two slits in the top of a roll to insert a cardboard tree. Paste on green paper leaves and brown paper

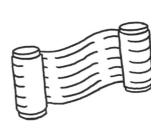

Scroll
Stick a long piece of paper to each roll.

Tall building
Paste on paper windows or add stickers.

Step 3: Design the overall package **page 83**

Craft ideas: *coloured patty cases*

Boat
Pinch either end.

Jewels on crown
Paste onto a strip of cardboard long enough to go around a child's head.

Lion face
Draw a lion's face in the centre.

Fish
Draw eyes and paste on tails. Alternatively cut patty cases in half to use as scales on a paper plate fish.

Flowers
Attach a straw or paddle pop stick as a stem. Cut the edge of the patty case to make petals.

Hat
Use as a hat on a cardboard roll puppet.

Hat
Cut or fold in half as a hat on a paddle pop stick puppet.

Hat
Paste the hat in such a way that it makes a sun hat for a paddle pop stick puppet.

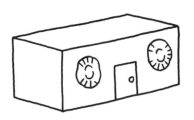

Windows
Paste on a tissue box house.

Eyes and mouth
Paste patty cases as eyes and fold a patty case in half to paste on as an opening mouth.

Skirt
Attach to a paddle pop stick puppet as a skirt.

Sun and moon
Paste a yellow patty case as the sun, cut and paste a white patty case as the moon. Add star stickers.

Craft ideas: *poly cups*

Puppet

Make a face puppet with round sticker eyes and paper streamer hair.

Cat

Paste on ears and face, draw whiskers.

Flower pot

Use it to grow a seed or seedling in dirt. Or make a flower to put in it.

Bell

Make a Christmas bell by threading a string through the middle and tying a bead on the end.

Pop up puppet

You can make a special puppet who hides inside the cup when you pull the dowel or straw stick.

Treasure cup

Decorate the outside and put treasures inside.

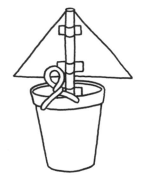

Boat

Attach a straw mast with paper sails and a pipe cleaner sailor.

Puppet

Wrap around clothes and/or arms. Paste on hair and add a face.

Craft ideas: *paper bags*

Puppet

Make a face puppet by pasting on facial features.

Treasure bag

Decorate and store something inside (eg. jigsaw pieces, memory verse).

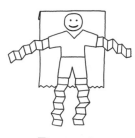

Puppet

Cut out and paste on clothes. Fold concertina strips of paper for legs and arms.

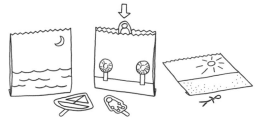

A scene

1) The sea: with boat inside.
2) Outside: patty case trees and green grass with puppets inside bag.
3) Desert: pipe cleaner person in bag.

Craft ideas: *milk/cream cartons*

Shaker

Put pasta inside, tape closed and decorate.

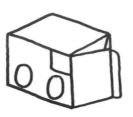

Car

Tape closed and paste on wheels and windows.

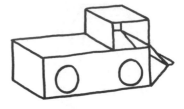

Truck

Tape closed, fold and attach cardboard as a cabin and add wheels.

Flower pot

Cut off the top of the carton to make a pot for planting seeds or seedlings.

Mobile

An adult will need to punch a hole in the top after it has been taped closed. Wrap around and paste a sheet of A4 paper for drawing on.

Peg box

Cut off the top of the carton. Peg on pictures, puppets or memory verses. Alternatively a pipe cleaner puppet could live inside.

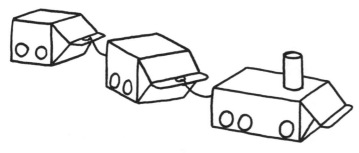

Train

Tape closed and paste on wheels and windows. An adult will need to punch holes so that the carriages can be joined together.

Buildings

Tape closed and paste on doors and windows.

Craft ideas: *egg cartons*

Caterpillar
Cut an egg carton in half length wise and decorate with stickers. Make antennae with flexi-straws.

Basket
Individual humps up-turned with pipe cleaner handles.

Bell
Individual hump covered with foil, and a pipe cleaner through the middle.

Treasure chest
Decorate the outside and put treasures inside (eg. shells, flowers and gum nuts).

Sea or desert
Paint the egg carton blue/yellow or cover with blue/yellow cellophane to make a wavy sea/desert with sand dunes. Put the boat in the sea or a pipe cleaner person in the desert.

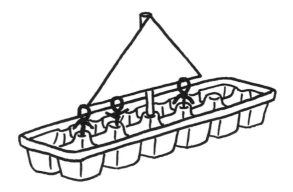

Boat
Use a straw for a mast. Make people with pipe cleaners.

A stand
Use a carton as a stand for a crowd scene of cardboard people.

Background
Use a carton as a background for scenery, eg. a paddle pop tree forest.

Craft ideas: *the humble peg*

Animal

Cut an animal body from cardboard and add pegs for ears and legs.

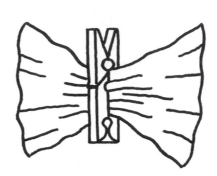

Butterfly

Cut a rectangle of crepe paper, scrunch up in the middle into the peg as the body.

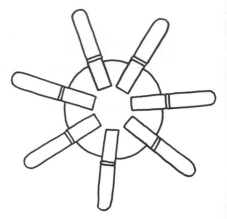

Flower

Add pegs as petals to a cardboard circle.

Peg leg Pete

Cut the body from cardboard and add pegs for arms and legs.

Mobile

Hang pictures on a coat hanger using pegs.

Wall hanging

An adult will need to cut holes in a sheet of cardboard. Use pegs in each hole to hold a picture.

Craft ideas: *straws*

Butterfly
Use two flexi-straws for the antenna.

Flag pole
Tape a piece of paper as a flag to a straw flag pole.

Flower stems
Either use patty cases as flowers or cut flower from cardboard. Tape straws to the back as stems.

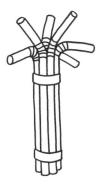

Tree
Tape a bunch of flexi-straws together so that the ends can bend out to make branches. You could add paper leaves.

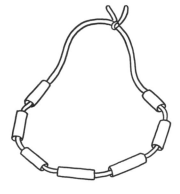

Necklace
Thread cut straws.

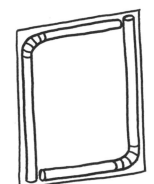

Frame
Use a strong glue to paste two flexi-straws in the shape of a frame.

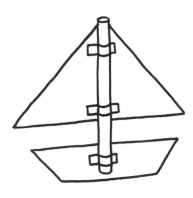

Mast
Tape cardboard sail and hull to a straw mast.

Legs
Cut an animal body from cardboard. An adult will need to punch holes for flexi-straw legs.

Puppet
Tape three straws together. Use one straw for the head and two bent straws for the arms.

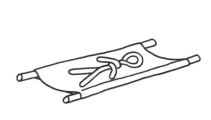

Stretcher
Tape or staple fabric or paper to two straws to make stretcher for a pipe cleaner person.

Tent pole
Use a straw as a tent pole, tape paper or fabric around it as the tent.

b. Action rhymes

Before you start thinking of action toys or nursery rhymes, let me explain what I mean. Something pre-schoolers love to do at pre-school is to learn little rhymes that have accompanying actions, usually just involving their fingers or hands. Young children learn these with enthusiasm and enjoyment, and they are quick learners. Action rhymes are particularly suitable for young children who can't read and find memory verses too hard to learn. They are also suitable for reinforcing a story and helping children remember it.

Action rhymes are a valuable resource for pre-school and Kindergarten Sunday School teachers to use. I would like to encourage you to have a go at writing them yourself. They are simply words that have an accompanying action. They don't have to rhyme, but they do need to be short with simple vocabulary.

i. Some sample action rhymes to get you started

God made my hands	*Hold up hands and shake them*
and I can clap them.	*Clap hands*
God made my feet	*Hands on feet*
and I can stamp them!	*Stamp feet*
God made my nose.	*Touch nose*
God made my toes.	*Touch toes*
God made each knee.	*Both hands on knees*
He made all of me!	*Arms outstretched*
God knows grown ups	*Hands high in air*
and every little baby.	*Cradle arms*
God knows children	*Point to each other*
and he knows me!	*Point to self*
(Repeat with the words "God made..." and "God loves...")	
God made the flowers	*Cup hands as a flower*
God made the butterflies	*Make butterfly wings with two hands*
God made the birds	*Put hands in the air as birds*
And God made me!	*Point to self*
God made my eyes.	*Touch eyes*
God made my nose.	*Touch nose*
God made my fingers,	*Wiggle fingers*
my ankles and toes.	*Touch ankles and toes*
God made my knees	*Both hands on knees*
and my elbows.	*Both hands on elbows*
God made all of me!	*Arms outstretched*

ii. Example action rhymes from a Bible story

Jesus calms the storm—Mark 4: 35-39

The disciples and	*Show 10 fingers and wriggle*
Jesus	*Show one finger*
were in a boat	*Cup hands to make boat*
and suddenly there was a storm.	*Boat on big waves*
The disciples were scared	*Fingers to mouth*
and Jesus said 'Stop'	*Hand stop sign*
and the wind	*Wave hands about*
and the waves	*Waves with hands*
were still.	*Hands still and flat*

Or a rhyming version

The waves were very big
and the strong wind blew
Then Jesus said 'Quiet'
the waves, and wind, stopped too.

Zacchaeus—Luke 19: 1-10 **(for older children)**

Zacchaeus was a short man	*Hold hand to indicate short*
and so he climbed a tree.	*Do climbing action*
Now above all the crowds,	*Put hand over eyes…*
Jesus, he could see.	*looking out*
Jesus stopped, looked up and said,	*Look up*
"I must stay in your house today".	*Make house outline with hands*
So Zacchaeus hurried down	*Jogging motion with arms*
and then went on to say,	*Outstretch arms*
"Half of my belongings	*Put one hand in middle of body*
I will give to the poor,	*Pretend to hand out a box*
and anyone I've cheated	*Shake head in remorse*
I will pay back, times four."	*Show four fingers*
Jesus said, "Salvation	*Arms outstretched*
has come here today."	*and again, with emphasis*
For Zacchaeus once lost	*Shake head with sad expression*
became God's child that day.	*Both hands on heart*

You guessed it: I'm going to ask you to write an action rhyme that would be suitable to teach your class. But you do have a choice—either write a rhyme for the next lesson that you are giving, or write one for your choice of the following passages. Remember, it doesn't have to rhyme, but it does need to communicate the main message:

▲ ● ■
HANDS ON EXERCISE: ACTION RHYMES

- Covenant with Abram—Genesis 12:1-3 (for older children)
- Jesus blesses the children—Matthew 19:13-15
- The great commandment—Mark 12:29-31
- Mary and Martha—Luke 10:38-42

c. Memory verses

Memory verses are a valuable way of helping children digest and remember biblical truths. Our aim in teaching Sunday School is to teach the Bible. We want them to know about God and how he wants us to live from his Word. Thus memorizing Bible verses is a valuable learning and reinforcement tool for children who are old enough to understand, read and remember the verses. Memorization without comprehension is a meaningless task. For children who are too young for memory verses, action rhymes and songs are an appropriate form for memorizing biblical truths.

A memory verse is in some ways a concrete piece of the Bible for a child. It's a bit that they can understand and remember—words that can be internalised, and provide assurance and direction. Bible verses show children what God thinks—how he wants us to live.

We want the children to see the Bible as our authority and guide. If a child learns the verse "Be kind" (Ephesians 4:32), then he will know that God wants him to be kind, not just the Sunday School teacher or parents, because it is in God's book.

Having said how valuable memory verses are, we should now consider how they are chosen and used. For memory verses must be chosen carefully, and it can be difficult sometimes to find verses that are appropriate. If you are using a manual that has memory verses included in it, then carefully consider the suitability of each verse before you teach it.

It is preferable to reduce the number of verses we teach and ensure that they are all suitable for the children and able to be learned and remembered.

Keep the following things in mind.

i. Context

The first thing to consider is the context of the verse. It is most unhelpful if we teach children a verse in which the original meaning has been tampered with by taking it out of context, omitting certain words or phrases or inappropriately applying it to a certain situation.

Key questions about the biblical context of a verse…
- Has the verse been taken out of context?
- If only part of the verse is learnt, does the portion of the verse being learnt convey the same meaning as the complete verse?
- Can we directly apply the verse to ourselves today? Where does the verse fit in the Bible's overall story? If it is an Old Testament verse, has its application changed in light of Christ?

ii. Translation

The translation of the verse should also be considered. Always aim to use the translation which is normally used in the class and with which the children are familiar. For simplicity reasons, we may find it easier to use other translations, yet it is important that we don't confuse children. If we teach them a verse from a different translation, they may find that the verse appears very different when they read it in their own Bible. We want to build their trust in the Bible and in us. So be consistent in your translation and make it clear that the verses are coming from your class Bible.

Given the above, it is important that you select a class Bible wisely. It needs to be a version with a simple vocabulary suitable for young children. (I tend to use the Good News Bible for Junior Sunday School). Remember that we want the children to see the relevance of the Bible to their lives today, and not be given the feeling that the Bible is too complicated or difficult to understand.

iii. Age level

A verse needs to be appropriate for the age and level of understanding of the children. Thus you need to think about…
- The language of the verse—is there any difficult vocabulary? Are there any difficult concepts?
- The meaning of the verse—what will the children understand the verse to mean? Is the meaning of the verse clear? Does the verse relate to the main message of the stories being taught?
- The length of the verse—is the verse too long for the children to remember?

iv. Memory skills

When considering the appropriateness of a verse, you also need to consider the memory skills of the children in your class. Some children find memorization easy and effortless. Other children find memorization difficult—try as they might, they just can't learn by memory. These are the children who can't learn their multiplication tables and whose spelling is often poor. These children need to feel comfortable in Sunday School without feeling threatened by memory tasks. For this reason it is best to avoid rewards for remembering verses, and not bring attention to academic performance. An ideal way to learn a verse is for all the children to say the verse together so that they help each other.

v. Presenting memory verses to learn

Do you have memories of teachers doing weird and wonderful things, maybe involving balloons or acrobatics, in order to teach a memory verse? Well, don't let those memories scare you off. There are ways of presenting verses without requiring circus tricks.

What you want is to have each word separately written so that they can be covered as the children learn the verse.

Here are some ideas:
- jig-saw puzzle—each word on a different puzzle piece
- word cards—call a child to the front to hold a card (with one word

from the memory verse on it). Continue so that you have a row of children holding cards. Children need to be moved so that their card is in the right place. Once the children are getting to know the memory verse, one child could turn their card around and everyone needs to guess the missing word.

- a code—give the children a simple code (e.g. '1' or '.-.' stands for 'a'). The children need to decipher the code to work out the memory verse. This is best for a short memory verse.
- a box—write each word on a different side of a box (if possible, a cube-shaped box). The children need to work out the correct order by rolling the box (a bit like a dice).
- a hat parade—each word is attached to or written on a paper hat, worn by children standing at the front. Individual children can turn around so that the 'hat' can't be read when the group is learning the verse.
- a spinning wheel—divide a cardboard circle into segments (one for each word). Cover (and join using a split pin) with another cardboard circle with one segment cut. Move the top circle to reveal the words, one at a time.
- shape 'find and match'—each word is written on a cardboard shape which is then hidden in the room. Once a child finds a shape he/she needs to match it on a master card out the front and attach it with Blu Tack so that the words are in the correct order.
- pass the parcel—a variation on an old theme. Instead of presents the parcel contains word cards and some little treats like jelly beans.

The list could go on and on. Try to come up with your own unique ideas!!

vi. Some possible memory verses

O LORD, our Lord, your greatness is seen in all the world!
(Psalm 8 verse 1)

The LORD is great. (Psalm 96 verse 4)

The LORD is king! (Psalm 97 verse 1)

LORD…you are ruler of all the earth. (Psalm 97 verse 9)

He made us, and we belong to him. (Psalm 100 verse 3)

The LORD is good. (Psalm 100 verse 5)

O LORD, you live forever. (Psalm 102 verse 24)

LORD, you have made so many things! How wisely you made them all!
(Psalm 104 verse 24)

The LORD is our God; his commands are for all the world.
(Psalm 105 verse 7)

Give thanks to the LORD, because he is good; his love is eternal.
(Psalm 136 verse 1)

The LORD is loving and merciful, slow to become angry and full of
constant love. (Psalm 145 verse 8)

Your rule is eternal, and you are king for ever. The LORD is faithful to
his promises. (Psalm 145 verse 13)

The LORD hates evil thoughts, but he is pleased with friendly words.
(Proverbs 15 verse 26)

Friends always show their love. (Proverbs 17 verse 17)

Pay attention to your teacher and learn all you can.
(Proverbs 23 verse 12)

Love one another. (John 13 verse 34)

Be kind. (Ephesians 4 verse 32)

or the full verse…

Be kind and tender-hearted to one another, and forgive one another,
as God has forgiven you through Christ. (Ephesians 4 verse 32)

Keep your lives free from the love of money, and be satisfied with what
you have. (Hebrews 13 verse 5)

And God showed his love for us by sending his only Son into the world,
so that we might have life through him. (1 John 4 verse 9)

▲ ● ■
TO DO

a. Over the next two weeks, as you read your Bible, look out for verses which would be suitable to use as memory verses. (If you happen to be reading a difficult part of the Bible, you could read some Psalms.)

b. If you teach school-aged children, choose one memory verse to teach your class over the next month. Decide how you will present it and teach it to your class.

d. Prayer

Prayer is a key part of the lesson and, like other parts, needs preparation. It is the time when we communicate with God, and, as such, should be approached with thought and care.

For children who have had no previous experience at home, Sunday School or Scripture, you will be modelling what prayer is; i.e. how to talk to God. For others who have had previous experience, you are reminding them of important truths about prayer—that talking to God is basic to our relationship with him; that we all can pray, at any time, anywhere, about anything.

i. How to pray

Prayer is something which children of all ages can do. Long before they can read the Bible by themselves, they can pray by themselves. It is important to give children the feeling that prayer is something that they can do. Therefore, the way we pray in Sunday School should be an example for the children to follow. We should use:

- simple language
- simple ideas
- short prayers.

The way in which you pray will depend on the age of the children and on their background, experience and level of confidence. The form of prayer may also differ according to the size of the group.

In order to keep our prayers simple and clear, it may be helpful to write notes beforehand on what you will pray about. When praying in front of a large group of children, it can be difficult to think clearly and pray fluently; and so writing your prayers, or notes on what you are going to pray about, can be beneficial. Praying in a class situation is a little different because we are praying in a much smaller group and with children we know.

Aim to pray naturally. If we do occasionally fumble for words or find ourselves being repetitive or stilted, then that is fine too. We are showing the children that we don't have to be articulate in order to pray, and that God hears us regardless of our literary expertise.

There are a number of questions that need to be answered when considering how you are going to pray. Here are some to think about:

- What will you call prayer (e.g. talking to God)?
- Will you ask for eyes to be closed? If so, what explanation will you give? For younger children you could ask them to close their eyes and put their hands together so that they will be able to listen better and not fidget.
- How can the children be involved in prayer?

ii. Praying with younger children (under 5 years)

Prayer with young children is essentially a matter of teachers modelling to the children how to pray and gradually giving the children more involvement as they grow older.

Here are some ideas for involving young children in prayer:

- The teacher praying aloud and all the children joining in saying "Amen".
- Children repeating one phrase at a time after the teacher (this may require a pre-written prayer so that each phrase of the prayer is short and easy for the children to remember and repeat).
- The teacher beginning a prayer and children adding a word or short sentence (e.g. "Thank you God for...").
- A time of discussion when the children mention things that they could thank God for or people they could pray for. This could be followed by the teacher telling each child how they could pray for what they suggested, or by the teacher briefly praying for these things.
- Pictures can be used in prayer. Before a prayer time, pictures could be drawn on a given topic (e.g. people we can pray for, food, things we can thank God for, things God has made, etc.). Children could say what is in their picture in the prayer time. You could even construct a little pictorial prayer book or prayer diary that enabled you to pray for different things, using pictures. For example, one page could be: "Thank you God for... (picture of trees and flowers)". Another could be: "Thank you God for... (picture of family)".
- Remember to keep prayers short—a few sentences at the most.

iii. Praying with older children (over 5 years)

Older children are usually more able to compose their own prayers with less intervention than with younger children. However, just because they have greater verbal skills doesn't mean they know how to pray. Children need to see us praying and learn from our example. Adult guidance and direction are important.

Here are some ideas for praying with older children:

- Pray after the story as a response to God's word (i.e. God speaks to us in his word, we can speak to him in prayer).
- Encourage children to pray natural, personal prayers. Discuss matters that you can pray about. Children won't always know how to pray about what they want to pray for. You may need to guide them.
- Model how to treat God. He is to be treated with respect and not to be approached like Santa or an automatic teller machine.
- Encourage children to pray by themselves at home. Perhaps even have times of quiet prayer in the Sunday School lesson when children can pray silently.

iv. What to pray with younger children (under 5 years)

There are different types of prayer, and we need to introduce the children to different ways of praying. The form that prayer takes will differ according to the age of the children

- Thank you God—remind the children of things that they can thank God for. Teach them to look at life with thankful hearts. Maybe when a child shares some good news, such as the birth of a baby brother or sister, you could respond with a comment like, "We can thank God for the baby".
- Praying for themselves and others—children are usually quite skilled at asking for things. Try to encourage the children to pray for other people as well as themselves. Teach them the ways that they can pray for others, particularly praying that God might help them. Also talk about things that the children can pray for themselves; e.g. asking God for help to be kind, to share their toys, to help their parents, to learn about God, and so on. Thus you are showing the children that God wants to help us but at the same time we are not to approach God as if he is a celestial Santa giving them everything they want.
- Sorry God—at an early age, children realise that they do things that they shouldn't do and that may be unkind. We can teach children to say sorry to God and each other. In a prayer time we could say something like, "Sorry God for all the things we do that we shouldn't do. Sorry for when we are unkind or hurt each other. Please help us to be kind to each other."

v. What to pray with older children (over 5 years)

- Thanking God—older children can more fully appreciate what God has done for them and given them. Try to channel their natural enthusiasm for life into thanks to God.
- Praying for themselves and others—encourage children to pray thoughtfully, thinking about how best they can pray for each other, their families, their friends and themselves. They can help others by praying for them. Encourage them to see the practical nature of prayer and the privilege of prayer; the fact that God wants us to pray to him. Also show them the types of things which they can be praying for themselves.
- It may be appropriate to give the children an opportunity to share prayer points before a time of prayer. For children who can read, it may also be appropriate for everyone to write down the prayer points so that they can be praying for each other through the week. In Sunday School you are showing the children how they can approach prayer themselves, so try to model helpful habits.
- Confession—older children are more aware of the consequences of their actions and the fact that at times they can be wilfully disobedient and unkind. We need to encourage them to be honest with God

and to help them realise that wrongdoings displease God. In a group prayer time it would be appropriate for the teacher to pray a general prayer something like this: "We are sorry, God, for all the wrong things that we do, for all the times when we are disobedient, unkind, rude and hurtful. Please forgive us for these things and help us to live the way you want us to. Thank you that you still love us." Children can be encouraged to be more specific in confession when they pray by themselves. Alternatively, there could be a time of silence when children can pray specifically.

vi. When to pray

Thought needs to be given to the placement of prayer in a lesson. What you want to pray will partly determine when you should be praying. Prayer that stems from the story may be best straight after the story.

One principle to keep in mind is that you want to pray when children are able to concentrate and take prayer seriously. It is not something to attempt when they are full of wriggles and mischief. We want to teach the children how to treat God, and that means giving him our full attention. You may want to try praying at different times in each lesson and see what seems to be the most suitable time. Remember that if you want the children to concentrate you need to limit the length of prayers. The younger the children, the shorter the prayers. One or two sentences are quite long enough for three-year-olds.

It is usually appropriate to pray more than once in a lesson. This will very much depend on the nature of the class and the age of the children. For instance, you might begin with a short prayer asking for God's help in listening and learning. A prayer may stem from the story. This might be a short prayer related to what the children have just heard. At a different time you might pray for others (each other, families, friends, missionaries, church members, etc.). I'm not suggesting that every part of the lesson is prefaced with prayer, but I am suggesting that we needn't be rigid about when and how to pray.

e. News time

Young children are gifted at being able to interrupt a story with a not-so-relevant piece of personal information. The younger the child, the less aware they are of socially appropriate behaviour and politeness. They are often eager to share their experiences with you and need to be gently instructed as to the most appropriate time to do this.

The introduction of a 'news time' in the lesson can be helpful. This provides an opportunity for children to share any personal news (e.g. their grandparents are visiting, they have a pet rabbit, they've got new shoes). However, it needs some care to make it work. Let me explain:
- Remind the children that when someone is talking they need to listen.
- Before you say the story, make it clear to them that it's your turn to talk and their turn to listen. If a child starts talking in the middle of

the story remind them that it's listening and not talking time and that they can talk later.

- Include news time in your class routine so that children are expecting it and know that there will be a chance for them to talk.
- When it's news time, remind the children that only one child speaks at a time and everyone else listens. You select the child to speak first. Discourage them from talking for too long.
- It's best if you select each child for their turn to share. If you do the selecting, the children will be more keen to behave appropriately while awaiting their turn.
- Respect the shy child. Children don't have to say anything. It's just an opportunity for anyone who wants to share something to do so at a suitable time.
- Encourage the children to listen (they will probably find it easier to talk than listen), especially those who have said their news.
- Ensure that each child speaks loudly enough to be heard.
- Discourage 'show and tell'; i.e. children bringing in things to show the class, as this can be very distracting. An action toy can take everyone's attention away from the lesson at hand. If children want to bring something in to show you, do so at the beginning of the lesson and then put it somewhere out of sight until the end of the lesson, or better still, give it to the parent to hold onto after you have looked at it.
- Thank everyone for sharing. Show them that you're interested in what they want to say. Help them see that it's worth waiting till news time to speak.

▲ ● ■
**CHALLENGE AND
CHANGE**

Reread this section on news time.
a. If you already have a news time, could it be improved by implementing some of the ideas mentioned? If so, list the ideas that would be helpful to introduce.

b. If you don't have a news time, is it something that you would like to introduce? How will you go about it?

Step 3b: Design the package

We're still not quite done yet! Many a wonderfully prepared lesson has fallen down at this point. You don't just need to think about what to do (content) but also how to do it (procedure) and how to move from one part of the lesson to another.

We've looked at all the different components that can be used to support and reinforce the teaching of the main message. Now you need to put these different components in the right order to make up the complete lesson. You need to know exactly what will be happening and when (think about how to prepare children for key concentration times, and how to vary active and passive times). Think about the links and how everything will fit together and flow. Then you can concentrate on the children during the lesson and not be distracted by your own preparations.

Here is the sample lesson format that I designed for my 'Zacchaeus' lesson (for a pre-school class):

- when children arrive—playdough or duplo
- clear playdough away and off tables
- go to group singing time
- stretching time
- sit on floor facing corner—finger games, touching head, toes, etc.
- introduction to story
- tell story with conclusion
- pray
- have sample activity to show and explain (what they will be doing and how it relates to the story)
- during this explanation another teacher sets up table for activity
- then recap by asking a question about the story: "What happened to Zacchaeus after he became Jesus' friend?"
- children sit at the table and do activities
- those finished early could draw or begin a second activity
- news time
- morning tea

Turn to Appendix A (page 185), where you've been working on the lesson for Luke 8. Drawing on the different components discussed above, design an overall package for the age group you have selected.

▲ ● ■
NOW YOU TRY

Chapter 7
Keeping control

In this chapter

1. Discipline

The word 'discipline' has negative connotations. It implies punishment. It brings to mind images of tears and wooden spoons. But discipline does not have to be viewed so negatively. It can be a positive way of helping children learn how to behave. If we can help prevent 'out-of-control' behaviour, then we will find that punishment becomes less of an issue. Prevention is certainly preferable to punishment.

How we manage our children is very important for their behaviour. We need to examine how we relate to the children in our class and see whether we are developing good management skills. Such techniques will assist in lessening difficult behaviour.

To make sure that there is an enjoyable learning environment for all of the children in your class, it is important that the teachers are not only in control but are seen by the children to be in control.

Remember: the essential thing is for the class to be able to hear and concentrate on the story. If one child's behaviour is preventing the others from hearing and learning about God then something needs to be done. By developing good management skills we are enabling the children to have the maximum opportunity to learn about God.

a. General principles of discipline

i.   Be in control of your class:
  - be observant and notice what's happening
  - be firm
  - expect respect
ii. Be loving.
iii. Aim to prevent rather than punish.
iv. Use positive reinforcement.
v.   Set clear guidelines for acceptable and unacceptable behaviour:
  - be consistent and fair in adhering to these
  - think beforehand of what threats you will make and when
  - remember to do what you say you'll do (don't make empty threats)
  - have class rules if appropriate
vi. Be well organized:
  - Know what you want to do when
  - Yet be flexible and adapt to their behaviour (provide concentration breaks if necessary)
  - Keep things moving
vii. Be responsible.

Let's look at each in more depth:

i. Be in control of your class

Children need to know who is in charge. And the person who is in charge needs to be in charge! By this I do not mean an ogre, but someone who is in control, who knows what should be happening and when it should be happening, who is observant (i.e. notices what's happening and responds accordingly), who is firm and who expects respect. This may sound like a tall order but it really isn't. If you are shaking in your boots, you simply need to appear calm and confident. Never let on to the children if you are feeling nervous. I suppose in some ways it's a matter of acting—being able to hide your insecurities and nervousness, and acting like you have been teaching for ten years and you are a teacher to respect.

Children will respect you if you are loving yet firm, and have made an effort to prepare well (showing the children that they are worth preparing for). They will have far more respect for you if you have clear guidelines for behaviour and are consistent in adhering to these, than if you let the class do anything and don't care how they behave.

Do not let the atmosphere in your class become chaotic and out of control. If the children start behaving in this way, put a stop to it immediately. You may need to stop whatever you are doing, and if necessary, move the children; for example, if they are climbing the walls and have started a paper throwing contest, you may need to get them all to sit down and do some other more beneficial activity. Concentrate on establishing calm.

ii. Be loving

In all our dealings with children under our care we should aim to be loving. God calls us to love others and this includes children, whether they are behaving themselves or not. We will find some children easier to love than others—some will have personalities that may appeal to us more than others. However, we are called to love them all. So aim not to have favourites, and do not act rashly. Always act responsibly and model to the children what it means to love others.

iii. Aim to prevent rather than punish

It is far preferable to prevent bad behaviour, than to have to punish it. You might respond by saying that it is impossible to prevent poor behaviour. To which I would say, yes and no. Children are sinners just like us, and we can't expect perfect behaviour. However, by getting to know the children in our class and by thinking through how they behave in different situations, we can minimise the likelihood of unacceptable behaviour. For instance, we need to make sure that we do not let the children become bored, tired or restless. Keep things moving, and maintain variety. We also need to get to know how the children behave in certain situations; e.g. what hypes them up? If we have an idea of what hypes them up, then we can try to prevent it happening. For more ideas to get you thinking there is a list of questions in chapter 15 under 'Evaluating Discipline'.

iv. Use positive reinforcement

Positive reinforcement means that you reinforce positive behaviour and therefore encourage the children to behave well. In a class situation it means using lots of praise. It means noticing positive behaviour and bringing attention to it—instead of only noticing poor behaviour and bringing attention to it. Children will soon learn that you notice positive behaviour (and they like to be complimented for their behaviour!). Remember to reinforce the sort of behaviour you want from them (be kind; listen; be a helper) rather than always telling them what you don't want (i.e. "Don't talk during the story").

v. Set clear guidelines for acceptable and unacceptable behaviour

Children, particularly young children, will not automatically know what is inappropriate behaviour. They may not realise that they shouldn't be standing on the chairs and tables (they may be allowed to do it at home). You need to tell them in clear terms what they are and are not allowed to do in your class at Sunday School. Once the children have a clear understanding of what is acceptable and unacceptable behaviour, then you need to be consistent and fair in adhering to these guidelines.

If (or when) the children misbehave, you need to act. It is appropriate to tell them to stop and then perhaps make a threat; e.g. "If you do that again then I will move you". It is a wise idea to think beforehand of what threats you will make and when, rather than being caught on the spot. At the beginning of the year, draw up a list of threats which progressively get stronger and decide in which situations it would be appropriate to use such threats. If you team teach, you will need to decide on these together. Then when you are faced with a misbehaving child in your class you will be able to respond appropriately. If the child continues to misbehave then you will know what to threaten next. Remember to do what you say you'll do—that means making threats that you are willing and able to carry out. Never make empty threats. Never threaten, for instance, to send a child out of the hall to be by themselves, since they are your responsibility and should be supervised at all times. The strongest threat might be something like sending the child to the superintendent or to a younger class (if appropriate). If you act immediately when a child misbehaves and make threats which the children would not like carried out, and if you then carry through on the promised consequences, the children will learn that you keep your word.

Use class rules if you think that it would be helpful. You may wish to have class rules if you find that the children regularly misbehave in the same way. By forming class rules you are clearly setting guidelines for appropriate and inappropriate behaviour. If you choose to have class rules:

- Have the absolute minimum—only two or three.
- Choose rules carefully (i.e. what you perceive to be key discipline problems).
- Phrase rules carefully. Be simple and concise, and phrase them positively rather than negatively; e.g. "listen" instead of "don't talk".
- Be consistent in adhering to your rules.

vi. Be well organized

It may sound like being organized has nothing to do with discipline. It does! It is important to know what you want to do and when. Have everything you need nearby so that you can concentrate on the children and keeping them under control. If your attention is distracted because you can't find your visual aids or you can't remember what to do with the children after the activity, then they will probably make the most of the opportunity! Have a structured routine (especially for younger children) so that the children clearly know what is happening when. Keep things moving and do not give them a chance to get up to mischief. It is also important not only to be organized but to be flexible and adapt to their behaviour. Provide concentration breaks if children are restless and make sure that you have their attention for the story.

vii. Be responsible

Never let your children out of your sight. Avoid hitting a child at all costs. If a child is being particularly difficult it is better to send them to the supervisor or to another class than do something that you will regret. We all have limits as to what we can put up with. Be wise in the way you treat children so that your actions are always above reproach. Do not touch children in a way that could be misread by someone (e.g. an affectionate hug is inappropriate). Sexual and physical abuse are a reality and we need to keep ourselves pure and be seen to be acting responsibly.

In summary, when relating to children remember to be:
- Consistent—so that children will clearly know the difference between acceptable and unacceptable behaviour.
- Positive—encourage, notice and praise good behaviour.
- Loving—treat children with loving care and carefully.
- Fair—don't bring attention to one child's misbehaviour and ignore another's.
- Firm—being firm is not contradictory to being loving.
- Honest—do what you say you'll do; no false promises or empty threats.
- Responsible—think of the safety and well being of your children.

b. An example of a discipline strategy when a child misbehaves

There are a number of effective strategies for 'classroom management' used by professional teachers in schools. Not all of these are suitable for a Sunday School (e.g. detentions!).

One frequently effective strategy suitable for Sunday School is the 'warn' and 'move' strategy (closely associated with the 'divide and conquer' strategy!), whereby you warn a child of the consequence if they continue to misbehave, then you carry out that threat. If a child does misbehave, show that this is unacceptable by telling the child to stop—and, where possible, explaining why it is unacceptable behaviour.

The successive threats to then use are basically to move the child:
i. to another place within the group (e.g. next to a teacher, and away from children who might be encouraging the bad behaviour by their reactions);
ii. to a place outside the group, but inside the class area (e.g. on a chair in a corner);
iii. completely away from the group (and the fun) by taking the child to the superintendent or a lower class (as long as there is an agreement with the teachers of that class).

This is very important: *Each of the above measures should be pre-empted by a warning*, such as: "If you do that again, you will have to go and sit over there".

Once you have given the warning, and the child misbehaves again, it is important that you *carry through on your threat*. (That, of course, means you should never threaten something that you can't or won't do.)

Please note: getting to step 3 is not a sign of failure on your part—it is a sign of failure on the part of the child to participate appropriately with the group.

c. Reconciliation

For more serious episodes of misbehaviour, the children should be encouraged to say 'sorry'—certainly to the teacher(s), but also to God. This is a chance to teach them about repentance and asking for forgiveness. If it is possible, pray with them—ask them to say a prayer first (not necessarily aloud), saying 'sorry' to God, and then you lead in prayer thanking God that they have realised that they need to change the way they have been acting, and asking God to help them.

It is important that as teachers you then extend your sincere forgiveness to them.

d. Some reasons why children misbehave (and some suggestions what to do)

There are many reasons why children misbehave. We often assume that children misbehave because they want to be disobedient and naughty, but that is not always the case. In fact, sometimes children may not consciously misbehave. Their inappropriate behaviour may be the result of unrealistic expectations on the part of the teacher. Children do have limited concentration spans; they do become restless; they are easily distracted and are quite capable of both frustration and boredom. So we perhaps need to see things through the child's eyes and think about whether our expectations are realistic and appropriate.

However, it is important to add here that children are skilled at being mischievous and naughty. When that is the case we need to act, making the children realise that certain behaviour is unacceptable.

I have outlined a number of reasons why children may misbehave or at least behave out of character. You will not always know why a child misbehaves, but there will be times when you will be able to identify contributing factors. This list is by no means exhaustive, but it will give you some idea of possible reasons behind poor behaviour. Once you have some idea of the reason behind a child's behaviour, and whether there is more to it than simply being naughty, you will be able to make decisions about how to respond to their behaviour.

Attention seeking
- Give them a lot of positive reinforcement when they're behaving well.
- Make it clear that you are interested in them as a person.
- Encourage, encourage, encourage…
- On the other hand, make it clear what is unacceptable behaviour— set clear limits within which they must behave. Be firm when they step out of line.

Discomfort
- Think about the conditions and whether the children are uncomfortable. If so, try to do something about it.
- Are the chairs too small, or the floor too hard?
- Are the children tired of sitting down?
- Are they too hot, or cold, or tired?

Distractions
- Look at things from the child's point of view. Are there things that would be distracting for a young child who is curious and who has a short concentration span? Children, on the whole, cannot block out distractions as easily as adults (and adults aren't all that good at it themselves!).
- Is a child facing a room full of other children and being distracted by what's going on? (Note: if you are wanting the children to give you full attention, for instance when telling the story, sit so that the children facing you see only a wall, and have their backs to the rest of the room/hall).
- Is one child annoying another child?
- Is the class next door too noisy?

Boredom

- Children do have a short concentration span (some shorter than others) and are easily bored.
- If boredom is a problem, try to add more variety to your class-time and make the activities as interesting as possible. Also think of alternative ways of doing things.
- Always over-prepare and not under-prepare. You are wise to have extra activities that can be called on if the children take less time than expected to do an activity.
- One child may be more advanced than the others, finish their work before everyone else and hence get bored easily. If so, try to give them more challenges and call on them to be a special helper. Make sure that you have activities for them if they finish early.

Not understanding

- Are the children simply not understanding what's going on?
- Is the story too complicated? If so, they may have given up trying to follow it.
- Were your instructions for the activity sufficiently clear?
- Are they unsure about what they are supposed to be doing? If it's possible that they have misunderstood you or they don't know what to do, then question them and repeat your instructions.
- Remember that some children are slower than others in their comprehension, memory, concentration, and listening skills. It is important for you to be patient.

Frustration

- A child may be frustrated because the given task is too hard for him. Try as he might, he can't do it adequately. Or the task may be based on his weakest skills (e.g. writing) which leads to frustration. If a child experiences repeated failure at school, then he will give up trying. We need to be on the lookout for such children and make Sunday School a caring, positive place to be.
- Far more children than we realise have learning problems or weaknesses in fundamental skills—they need to feel that they can achieve, and are accepted for who they are and not what they can or can't do.
- If a child is frustrated then you may need to change the nature of his/her activity. Can you change it so that they don't have to do all the writing? Can you make the task less frustrating for them?
- If you have problems because a child is repeatedly feeling frustrated, then you may need to change the nature of the activities each week so that they are more suited to that child. It will help that child feel more positive if he/she can join in and do what everyone else is doing. Bring the least amount of attention as possible to the child's weaknesses.

Immaturity

- Are you expecting your children to be nine-year-olds when they are four? (Remember that the younger the child, the more restless he will be). You may need to reread chapter 2 about the characteristics of each age group and check that your expectations are realistic.
- If one child is noticeably younger or more immature than the rest, then make sure that you are catering for them. If they seem socially inexperienced (a common problem among children who haven't started school yet), then make it clear to them what is acceptable and unacceptable behaviour. Keep them beside a teacher where possible, especially in a group activity, so that the teacher can keep an eye on them and guide them in their behaviour.

Restlessness

- There are a variety of reasons why children may be restless (some have already been mentioned). If the children are restless, then remember to break up sitting activities with activities that require movement, thus giving their bodies a chance to wriggle and stretch. This may mean simply stretching, doing something standing up or walking around (in a carefully controlled way).
- If your children become quite restless, then you may need to do a brief activity specifically designed to get rid of wriggles. The appropriateness of such activities will depend on the age of the children. Use your imagination, but don't do anything that will make the children be silly. See 'Concentration Breaks' below for some suggestions.

Weather

- Believe it or not, the weather does affect children's behaviour, especially wind, rain and heat. If it has been raining for days, then remember that the children will be quite restless—they are not fond of being pent up inside for days on end. On windy days, children can also be very restless. On hot days they may find it difficult to concentrate.
- Make sure that you vary active and passive activities.
- If it is hot, then preserve their energy as much as possible and reduce their concentration time if possible.
- See above (under Restlessness) for further suggestions.

Hyperactivity

- Some children are hyperactive, or may become hyperactive in certain situations. If a child does have a real problem then his/her parents should give you prior warning, and advise you on appropriate strategies.
- Calm the child down as much as possible.
- Lower, rather than raise, your voice.
- Do active movements (to release pent-up energy) that gradually calm down and flow into a quiet activity.

Allergies

- Don't give children food containing high levels of sugar or additives (e.g. MSG)—be on the safe side.
- If a parent tells you of a child's allergy, then write it down. Take such information seriously.
- A child may have been to a party the day before or eaten something on the way to Sunday School which has hyped him up. In such cases the best thing that you can do is to break up sitting or high concentration activities with active movements (see above). Unfortunately, you have no control over what they have done prior to Sunday School.

'Behind-the-scenes' problems

- If a child behaves quite uncharacteristically, then there is often a hidden problem, such as family trauma, or illness.
- Be sensitive and caring.
- Make sure that other children in the class are not being unkind.

Just plain naughtiness

- Children and adults alike are sinful.
- When children are being naughty for the sake of it, be firm and make them realise that their behaviour is unacceptable (see the 'general principles' above).
- Remember: if parents send their children to Sunday School, then they usually want them to listen and learn. If a child's behaviour continues to be a problem, it is wise to tell their parents. A word from his/her parents before Sunday School may transform his/her behaviour. In the case of a real, ongoing problem a parent could be asked to sit with the class.

▲ ● ■

THINK AND PRAY

a. *Patience and self-control are two of the most difficult attributes to develop when working with children. Are you trying to be patient and self-controlled when dealing with the children? Pray about these two fruits of the Spirit that they might grow in your lives.*

b. *When a child misbehaves, do I over-react and become too easily angered? Do I under-react and allow children to disrupt others by continuing in mischievous acts?*

c. *When I discipline, am I fair and consistent?*

d. When relating to the children, am I positive and responsible?

e. Do the children in my class know the boundaries for acceptable and unacceptable behaviour?

f. What changes do I need to make? How am I going to make them?

Discipline Strategy

The purpose of this exercise is to consider the most appropriate discipline strategy for your situation. Look back over the material above, think about your own situation, and devise a discipline strategy for your class by completing the exercise below.

▲ ● ■
THINK AND DO

a. Our strategy for aiming to prevent misbehaviour problems:

(e.g. notice and praise appropriate behaviour, encourage children where possible, provide opportunities for children to wriggle and squirm, variety between active and passive activities)

i. _____

ii. _____

iii. _____

b. Statement of appropriate and inappropriate behaviour

i. Appropriate behaviour (that we want to encourage)
(e.g. listen when someone is talking, be kind, be helpful)

_____

_____

ii. Inappropriate behaviour (that we want to discourage)
(e.g. throwing, swinging on chairs, hitting, bad language)

_____

_____

c. Series of threats for unacceptable misbehaviour

(e.g. move to another place within the group, move to a place outside the group but within class area, take the child to the superintendent)

i. _____

ii. _____

iii. _____

d. Sunday School statement regarding behaviour (to have displayed in hall)

(phrase this carefully—simple, concise and positive rather than negative; e.g. "At Sunday School we listen, we are kind and we are helpful")

_____

_____

2. Concentration breaks

What is a concentration break? It's a short space of time when you do something with the children that is completely different and provides them with a break in concentration. Concentration breaks are useful in keeping children from becoming restless and enabling them to concentrate better for the story (or some other time you want them to listen attentively).

a. Ideas for younger children

i. Using hands

Hands are easy to move, and you can move them while still sitting down.

- Shake hands—up high, down low, in front of you, behind you.
- Clap hands along with the teacher.
- Touch heads, shoulders, knees, and—a little harder—elbows, wrists, ankles.
- Make your hands into an animal chosen by the teacher; e.g. a mouse which creeps up your arm, down the other arm and into your lap and goes to sleep (this is an ideal, short break which slows and quietens at the end).
- Reach for the ceiling, walls, or floor.

ii. Using fingers

Moving fingers is fun. Let your imagination think of different things your fingers can do, like dancing and running. Children enjoy the variety and the challenge.

- Make them dance, march, run, creep.
- Be the wind, rain.

iii. Other

- Sing an action song.
- Pretend to be a… (e.g. rock).
- Do what I'm doing (children copy the teacher's actions).

b. Ideas for older children

i. While sitting

- Do what I'm saying not what I'm doing (try to trick the children; e.g. by saying "touch your elbows" while you are touching your head).
- Clapping sequences; e.g. two claps with hands, one on shoulders and one on knees and repeat (children do the sequences with you—this can be quite a challenge).

ii. While standing

Keep control. Give specific directions that the children need to follow. Always direct the children from the moment they stand up. If you simply tell them to stand up and wiggle they will probably go very silly.

- Be a pencil (arms by sides and still), and then as a contrast be a tree in the wind and then back to a pencil.
- Everyone do two hops on one foot and now three hops on the other foot. Jump three times, touch your toes twice. Touch your shoulders, touch your elbows, touch behind your knees and now sit down.

iii. Guessing games

Begin giving clues which could be true of lots of people, animals or things, and gradually make your clues more specific so it becomes a challenge to guess the right answer.

- "I'm thinking of someone God has made who has a hose, is very dirty, usually has a bucket, wears gloves…" Keep giving clues until they guess (a gardener).
- "I'm thinking of something big that grows near the ground. It's green on the outside… (pause) and pinky red on the inside… (pause) with seeds" (a watermelon).
- You can also combine the descriptions with mime: "I'm thinking of someone who does lots of different things. They wear uniforms and something they do is…" [mime directing the traffic] (a policeman/woman).

c. Some general pointers

- Keep control of the children at all times—you direct the children in what they are doing.
- If you want children to sit and keep listening after the concentration break, then be careful if you have children standing up as it can be difficult to settle them down again.
- With older children, vary your concentration breaks so that they themselves don't become boring and predictable. The unpre-

dictable will generate interest and keep them focussing on you (and less likely to misbehave).

· When doing actions, always do quiet, slow actions towards the end. Children may begin touching heads, then toes, etc. but then touching shoulders…elbows…knees. Now you have their hands quietly in their laps where you want them!

3. Using puppets

One of my favourite friends is called Minty Monkey. He often accompanies me when I teach (children and adults alike!). It doesn't take him long to win everyone's heart and to have children look longingly into his eyes. Minty seems to have a charisma that we would only dream about having. Minty is a puppet, a piece of fur fabric that has developed a personality all of his own.

Another friend of mine is called Jasper. He is also a puppet, but he is on a stick (see illustration). Jasper appears when children are quiet, but as he is shy, he quickly goes into his little home if children are too noisy. Once a seven-year-old boy was so captivated by Jasper, he asked me if Jasper was real.

On one occasion when I didn't have a puppet with me, the only thing I could find was a post-it note (a square piece of paper with a sticky strip on the back so it can stick to things). It became Mr Square and the children drew eyes, nose, a mouth and hair so Mr Square could have an identity all of his own. The children were fond of him because they helped to make him. Mr Square could stick on the board wherever we wanted him to be. He was most cooperative and helpful!

Unfortunately, adults get scared when I talk about using puppets. They feel nervous, saying that they are not good at that sort of thing and that they wouldn't know what to do with it. What many adults don't realise is that they can have no acting talent and laryngitis and a puppet could still work. Why? Because children make puppets work. Children are naturally attracted to puppets. They will quickly forget all about you and totally focus on the puppet that is an extension of your hand. None of my puppets talk aloud—they just whisper in my ear and I tell the children what they have said. So I don't need to have skills at accents and ventriloquism, which is just as well, because I don't!

When you use puppets you need to work within your limitations. If you can't do accents then have whispering puppets. If you can't do expressions and actions then use a puppet like Jasper which lives with one permanent expression on his face.

I don't really want to have a list of guidelines as to when, how, and where to use puppets. In many ways it's an individual thing. How I use a puppet may be completely different from how you would use a puppet. If I tell you my way, then there's a chance you will change your way to be like mine, when yours is actually better for you.

So rather than a list of do's and don'ts, I will share with you a few ways in which puppets can be used:

- To help with 'crowd control' a puppet might only come out when everyone is quiet, quickly retreat when the children become noisy, and only reappear when everyone is suitably quiet.
- A puppet might whisper questions in your ear which you then repeat out loud. This may become an introduction or conclusion to a story.
- The puppet can listen to the story with the children. So the puppet sets an example to the children how to listen (I have observed that puppets are very obedient and are excellent students; they always listen attentively and don't interrupt). Alternatively, the children can show the puppet how to listen to the story (and let's hope that they set a good example—at least the puppet is a good motivation).
- The puppet can help tell the story or be a character in the story (see chapter 5 on visual aids for more help here).
- There can be a class puppet who is in the class each week (he could even have other puppets visiting him). The possibilities are endless.

To give us some idea of what can be used to make a puppet, who better to enlighten us than a child. My daughter made a puppet when she was about six years old. It was to be a bridegroom for her 18-inch tall doll. She used a cardboard box, but not how I imagined it to be used. The sides of the box were cut up and one became the body; others were used for the arms (with fingers too) and legs. The limbs were joined onto the body with string (Mum made the holes). A paper plate was used for the face. Then the groom was dressed in a black suit using old black stockings and a skivvy. She found an A4 page of paper to be the perfect size for his shirt and proceeded to draw buttons down the front. A real flower was put in his top pocket and the final touch was a ring, placed on one of his fingers. The wedding was a happy occasion and Naomi, Lauren's doll, seemed pleased with her handsome groom!

Need more puppet ideas? Re-read Step 2c (page 56) on illustrating the story in chapter 5.

Further resources and suggestions for improving discipline in your class are contained in chapter 15, 'Evaluation'.

Go into the kitchen and find something which inspires you as a potential puppet. With the cook's permission, and a little imagination, see if you can create a puppet. You might like to take your new friend to Sunday School. If you are doing the training sessions you will be having a puppet display.

▲ ● ■
THINK AND DO

4. Where to now?

That completes Part 1, and the basic skills of Sunday School teaching. There is, of course, plenty more to learn. Part 2 contains all sorts of interesting information, some of it more relevant to the superintendent or co-ordinator of the Sunday School, but some of it very relevant to you, the teacher. In particular, make sure you take a look at:

· chapter 11 on safety and toilet troubles
· chapter 14 on getting organized
· chapter 15 on evaluation

Part 2

More resources for Sunday School teaching

Running a Sunday School is a complex and demanding job. In the following chapters, we will look at everything from what to do when the children first arrive, to how to train teachers. If you are a Sunday School superintendent or part of a leadership team, Part 2 is especially for you. (Part 2 also contains plenty of useful information that all teachers should read, particularly in chapters 11, 14 and 15.)

Chapter 8

The location

In this chapter

How to make the most of your location

We usually don't have much control over the choice of location for Sunday School. It tends to meet in whichever room or building is available. Since it might not be the ideal location, this can make the task of teaching difficult. In my experience, most Sunday Schools have some problem with their location, but rather than having a negative attitude which hampers the functioning of Sunday School, teachers need to be creative and flexible in their thinking.

We want Sunday School to be a fun, positive place for the children, and it helps if the room is enjoyable to walk into. If you're currently stuck with dim lighting, peeling walls, and tattered old carpet, start thinking creatively about inexpensive ways to brighten the atmosphere.

Primarily, it needs to be safe, clean and tidy. If you can't change the room in any other way, at least ensure that it is these three things. Safety is of utmost importance. If there are any dangerous things in the hall (e.g. broken furniture, ladders, tins of paint or chemicals, timber boards with nails poking out etc.) they need urgent attention. Hopefully, there will be someone responsible for maintenance in the church who could attend to these problems. If the area is used for other activities through the week, some teachers may have to arrive early on a Sunday so that the room can be tidied.

The next change which may need to be made is the addition of colour. If your room is rather drab, with an odd assortment of furniture, then it would help if it could be brightened up. If it is appropriate in your situation, buy a combination of blue, yellow, red and green paint and paint the furniture. It's amazing how a few bright colours can change the atmosphere of a room. Colourful curtains are also a great addition—each curtain could be a different primary colour; or you may find some inexpensive, appropriate curtain fabric at a bargain fabric shop; or you may be able to paint or dye calico (an inexpensive cream coloured fabric) to use for curtains.

If you have large expanses of bare walls, murals and posters can be made by the children. Calico can be painted, or a collage picture can be made from fabric scraps and felt glued on to it. The advantage of murals made by the children is that they feel as if they have had a special part in the decoration of their room.

Cubicles or class areas can be decorated with work made by the children of that class. Even timber partitions or large cupboards can be decorated in such a way.

What do you do if you can't leave the children's work on the walls? My suggestion would be to staple their work on to a large piece of hessian or calico and hang this up each week, and then roll it away afterwards.

To highlight the importance of having a bright, colourful room decorated with the children's work, I'd like you to think back to classrooms you were in as a student at school. Infants classrooms tend to have an uplifting feeling as they are full of colour, decoration and interest. Secondary School classrooms, however, can often be devoid of colour and interest, and feel uninspiring to walk into. Remember?

Pretend you have never been to your Sunday School hall/room/cubicle before. Walk in and look around.

a. What does it look like?

b. How does it feel to walk into?

c. Do changes need to be made?

d. If so, how could changes be made given your circumstances and budget?

e. If no changes need to be made, then enjoy your surroundings!

Chapter 9

When children arrive

In this chapter

1. The atmosphere (what they feel)

The atmosphere of your Sunday School needs to be welcoming, friendly and caring. This applies to the people as well as the room. Bright smiles and friendly faces make an impression on first-timers to a Sunday School, and are a great incentive for children to return. If a child enters a Sunday School building knowing he/she will be warmly greeted by his/her teacher and able to talk about his/her week, then he/she is likely to be eager. If the child also knows that he/she will have an enjoyable time at Sunday School, then there is even more reason to be eager.

The role of the class teachers is important here. They need to be free from other responsibilities and distractions (like last minute preparations) so that they can greet the children and talk to them.

I realise that in some Sunday Schools children go to church beforehand. In this case, some of the following will not be relevant to you.

2. A welcomer (who they meet)

For newcomers

It is valuable to have someone assigned to the job of welcoming newcomers. This will often be the superintendent, but it may be a teacher's role to greet people as they arrive. A key aspect of the job is simply to **notice newcomers** and then to greet them accordingly. Both children and parents alike need to feel at ease when going to Sunday School for the first time. It is important that they be met as soon as possible after walking in the door. Be warmly welcoming and remember that it may be the first time that the parent and child have ever set foot in a church building. You want them to feel as comfortable as possible.

The welcomer should have a list of children and classes readily accessible so that they know which class to direct a new child to. It is important for a child to be placed in the right age group on their first visit (particularly pre-school children). If a child is placed in the wrong class on the first visit it can make it very difficult to move to a different class later. Some children unknowingly stay with the wrong age group, and it isn't picked up until they start school. Please ensure that this doesn't happen.

Many young children find it difficult to be separated from their parents in a new environment. If a child is clingy, ask the parents what would be best for that child (i.e. for the parent to leave or stay). If the parent chooses to stay make sure that you make them feel as comfortable as possible. Just imagine a shy parent coming to church for the first time in their life and finding themselves sitting in a room full of children with the only other adults present being young, vibrant Sunday School teachers (does that sound like you?)! It can be as daunting for the parents as it is for the children.

For the regulars

The need for a welcomer applies equally to children who attend regularly. Many young children find it difficult to enter a large building with lots of people inside. It is very daunting for them, and being wrapped around Mum or Dad will seem far more secure than being alone in a big room.

Please remember to greet all children warmly, especially those who are shy or insecure. It is also wise to provide a familiar face at the door, rather than a different teacher each week. When shy/insecure children arrive, it will help enormously for them to see the same person they always see as they arrive at the door. They can be helped to their class, where the teacher can take over.

3. Initial activities (what they do)

When children arrive at Sunday School, it is important that they know where to go and have something to do. It is also important for there to be a calm, organized atmosphere without an air of chaos. There needs to be a regular routine: children and parents need to be clear about where to go, and activities need to be set up for children to do when they arrive, as their arrival times will vary and you can't expect young children to sit and wait for everyone to arrive. When waiting for children to arrive, don't sit blankly staring into space—start an activity to help draw children in. It is helpful if children can see something happening that they can join in with when they first arrive.

There are two alternative arrangements for when children arrive. They could go straight to their individual cubicles or to group activities set up at tables. Suitable activities for either situation would be blocks, puzzles, reading books, playdough, drawing or colouring.

a. Class cubicles

The advantage of initial activities being in their own cubicles is that children are in a familiar, secure environment with teachers they know. There is the opportunity for informal conversation, which is valuable for building a relationship with the children. Also, if children meet in their class cubicle, they could help with preparation for the group time or lesson; e.g. they could do some pasting or colouring on the visual aid for the story, or draw pictures of things to pray for or thank God for. They will have added interest in the story if they have been involved in preparing the visual aid.

b. Group activities

If you have this arrangement, different tables are set up in the hall with a different activity on each. The children choose where they want to go based on what they want to do. One table might have playdough set up;

another table might have puzzles. The advantage of this arrangement for the children is the element of choice, and from the teacher's point of view, it probably involves less preparation. However, if you have this arrangement it is important that the children can easily find their class teachers.

4. Considering construction toys

One type of toy that I find effective as an initial activity is what is often called a construction toy. This includes a variety of models and makes of plastic bits and pieces (like straws, rings, sticks, blocks etc.) that fit together to make all sorts of things. I like such toys because they are creative (there is no right or wrong way) and they can be worked on as a group. Children might choose to work together—like a year 2 class which specialises in making the highest construction possible using straws which interlock. Alternatively, some or all children can work individually. So children can join the group at any time without missing out.

Another reason why I encourage the use of these toys is that children don't need to give their full attention to the task and they can talk at the same time. In fact, children are more likely to talk if their fingers are busy than if they are sitting still feeling like a spotlight is on them. (Just as an aside, I have found that many boys benefit from a relaxed environment like this in order to open up and talk.) This is a wonderful opportunity to talk with the children in your class, get to know them better and have fun together. Teachers will enjoy being big kids for a while and with an interactive construction toy, teachers and children alike are on the same level. And as it comes right at the beginning of Sunday School while children are arriving, it is not taking up time which could be spent on the lesson.

5. Conclusion

Whatever you choose to do, make sure that the initial activities set the appropriate mood for the lesson to follow. Don't hype children up to the extent that there is no chance of them settling down to concentrate at a later stage. It is also important that the children feel a sense of belonging and purpose as they arrive, and are not left to themselves. If they start feeling bored at this stage it can be very difficult to overcome. So ensure that there is something (and someone) waiting for the children as they arrive.

a. The teacher

- *Are you ready when children arrive? If not, what steps are you going to take to change?*

- *How would you rate your greeting of children when they arrive? How might you improve?*

b. The activity

- *How effective are the initial activities you use?*

- *How much do the children enjoy doing them?*

- *Are there any problems? If so, what are they?*

- *Do any changes need to be made? If so, what changes will you try to implement and how?*

Chapter 10

The group time

In this chapter

1. What is the group time?

In many Sunday Schools there is a group time before the children break up into classes. This group time is invariably towards the beginning of Sunday School after the initial activities. It is often very difficult to run successfully as it comprises such a wide range of ages. A Junior Sunday School may have children from 2-8 years; a Senior Sunday School may have children from 8-12 years; and a combined Sunday School may have an age range spanning both groups. So you will find that the attention span, interests and abilities of your youngest and oldest children will be vastly different.

However, before I sound too negative, there are many positive reasons for having a group session. Firstly, it helps establish and build the unity of the Sunday School. Children realise that they are a part of a wider group. It provides an opportunity for the children to sing together. It can also be a suitable time for memory verses, news time, prayer and even drama. It is also a great time to acknowledge birthdays and to sing 'Happy Birthday'.

2. Who should run it?

I would encourage you to have the same person leading the group time each week. This is a great help to its smooth running. The leader can build a rapport with the group, establish a method of managing discipline, and gain the respect of the children.

Children need routine and, to some extent, familiarity. (I'm sure that you can all recall the treatment that relief teachers received at school as opposed to the regular class teacher.)

3. How should it be run?

This will largely be determined by the individual situation of each Sunday School (e.g. number of children, age range, number of teachers, availability of musicians, etc).

However, certain principles should apply:
- The teacher needs to be organized and well prepared. Have a list of the order of songs, make sure the song sheets are easily accessible, give the pianist/guitarist the song list, and so on.
- Seat the children in a tight group with the leader close to the children and near their level (i.e. not standing while everyone else is seated on the floor unless the group is particularly large). Rapport is far easier if you are close to the children.
- Eye contact—the big principle in seating arrangements should be

that all children need to be within view of the leader. Have no hidden corners. A large Sunday School may have the children sitting in a group. A smaller Sunday School may have a circle. Either way it is essential that everyone can see, and be seen by, the leader.

- Have a general outline which you usually follow. Include calm activities or songs towards the end of the session so that the children are in an appropriate mood to go to their classes.

- Be flexible—which doesn't mean disorganized. There are many factors which affect the success of a group time but that you will never be able to predict: the weather, the general mood of the children, the number of latecomers, and so on. It is important that you are able to adapt to the situation at hand. You may need to change the order of songs because of the children's mood, or even omit a song.

- Teachers sitting among the children need to be trained to be actively involved and not passive onlookers. They are not there to be entertained. Rather, they should be aware of what is happening around them, helping to control the behaviour of the group and participating in actions and singing (remember that children will imitate adults). Teachers should be seated throughout the group of children (rather than sitting in a row at the back) and preferably sitting with children they know. However, if the teachers are preventing other children from seeing because of their size, they may need to sit at the sides of the group. If they notice a child being disruptive it should be their responsibility to act, instead of waiting for the leader to act. It is far preferable for misbehaviour to be quietly and discreetly dealt with rather than the whole group being disrupted. It should be a last resort for the leader to bring attention to a child's misbehaviour. I might add at this point that the leader doesn't have omni-vision, and while he or she may notice one child's misbehaviour he/she may not be aware of another child being equally as mischievous.

- Provide space for latecomers. It is often difficult for families to leave home at a given time. Children have a variety of spontaneous, unintentional stalling habits (some, though, may be intentional!) such as missing articles of clothing, uncombed hair, and so on. Please allow room for latecomers to be able to join the group easily with the least amount of distraction to the group. In a large Sunday School you may find the need for a teacher to stand at the door and direct late children.

- The group session should not be too long. It's far better to be short and dynamic, than long and boring. Remember that young children have a short concentration span.

- It is important to establish an orderly routine for the children to return to their classes. It is best if the children go to their cubicles one class at a time, rather than in a chaotic and noisy mass. The mood in which they go to their classes will carry over into the lesson so the group leader needs to insist on quiet, orderly behaviour. The leader might ask the children to 'creep' to their classes.

4. What should the programme be?

This will largely depend on the size, age and make-up of the group.

For Junior Sunday Schools, the group time will mainly be singing. Young children enjoy singing, and it is a great way of teaching them biblical truths in a form they will remember. See 'Singing' below.

Prayer is valuable in a group time. The group leader could say a prayer which is either repeated by the children line by line, or the children could join in saying "Amen". Alternatively, some of the children could come out the front to participate in prayer. They may say a word or a line, or they may show pictures which were drawn during the initial activities time. The group leader could begin a prayer with "Thank you God for..." and the children say one word each (e.g. food, water, families, friends etc.) when the leader taps them.

Memory verses could be learnt in the group time. Care needs to be taken in the choice of verses that would be suitable for such a wide age group. See chapter 6 for more details on memory verses.

An occasional segment on missionaries is a great idea. If your church supports missionaries, include an update on their news or simply remind the children of them, and pray for them. If you are able to obtain some photos of the missionaries, it would be helpful to show these as you talk about them.

News time is another possible activity. For it to be effective it needs to be well organized. Only have about three children saying news. Choose them at the beginning and let them come out the front to share their news. They will have to be encouraged to speak loudly and to the group. The group leader may need to ask questions to encourage them to speak. The one problem with news time in the group time is that 20 or 30 children cannot share in the one group time! You may prefer just to have birthday children coming out to share.

News time can end with a birthday song for all the birthdays in the week. It is important to keep an accurate and up-to-date roll so that you know who is having a birthday.

5. Singing

Songs fulfil a range of aims. They are enjoyable, memorable and helpful for children. Never underestimate the potential of songs as a learning and reinforcement tool.
· Children find songs easier to remember than words alone.
· Children can learn songs quickly.
· Songs reinforce a message.
· Songs are enjoyable.

a. Selecting songs

Much care should be taken when choosing songs for children. We need to ensure that the lyrics are truthful and helpful, as our young singers won't necessarily be able to discern things that are not quite right.

Don't be attracted just to catchy tunes with fun actions. Lyrics are very important. I fear that too often we choose songs because they have fun bits in them and appealing actions, and we give little regard to their words. The words may be inappropriate because the vocabulary is too difficult for the children to understand, or it may be that the song-writer has simplified biblical truths in an inaccurate way. Songs must use vocabulary and concepts that the children can understand. The meaning must be clear, without unhelpful or ambiguous phrases.

However, if a song is generally suitable but it has a difficult word or phrase, preface the singing with a simple explanation.

We also need to remember that short catchy songs with fun actions and good words will be remembered better than good words with boring music and no actions! [1]

Remember to respect copyright and follow the guidelines of the publishers.

b. Singing with pre-schoolers

Songs are a particularly effective learning tool for pre-schoolers. They can't read or write, but they can sing, and they have fantastic memories for songs that they like.

- Songs need to be:
  - simple
  - short
  - clear
  - repetitious
  - easy to understand (no difficult words or concepts)
- Consider the length of songs. The shorter the song, the more quickly and easily it will be learnt (which is particularly important for younger children who haven't learnt to read yet—they will be singing from memory). For younger children, avoid songs with numerous verses, unless they are fairly repetitive (i.e. only changing a few key words in each verse).
- Children (especially younger ones) enjoy repetition. Don't be afraid to repeat songs several times in a session.
- To introduce some variety, sing the same song a few different ways: using clapping or actions, breaking into parts, loudly/softly, fast/slow, with/without simple percussion instruments, and so on.
- Actions are valuable because they aid memory; they are fun for the children and they encourage participation.

c. Singing with school-aged children

Unfortunately, the secular music industry often captures our children at a young age. In a child's mind, the songs sung at Sunday School can seem very old-fashioned in comparison. Fortunately, there are a growing number of Christian artists writing and recording songs which are appealing to children, and which work against the 'old-fashioned image' of Christian songs. Look around for modern music. You need to be prepared to hunt! And once you think you have found an ideal solution, read the lyrics carefully.

If you find a worthwhile song to teach, try to think of actions that could accompany the song. If a song has biblical, helpful lyrics there are many ways that you can make it more appealing to school-aged children by adding actions or facial expressions.

d. Writing a song

If you can't find a suitable song then you may be able to write one. Before you decide that you would never be able to, remember that:

· the tune need only be very basic
· familiar tunes can be used and you need only think of the words
· for young children, the simpler the song the better
· the words don't have to rhyme
· you don't need accompaniment in order to sing (more on this later)
· if you do have a pianist or guitarist, then they could work out the appropriate chords

e. Example for two- to four- year-olds

Let's say that the message you want the children to learn from a particular lesson is that God loves them and that this is a cause for happiness. Here's how we could write a song to reinforce that message.

Message: God loves them. This is a cause for happiness.

Words: God loves me
           God loves me
           I can be happy for
           God loves me.

Tune: Think of a simple tune, such as the simple three note tune below.

Alternatively, you could put the words to a familiar tune (Note: by this I don't necessarily mean a tune which the children know—so long as you know the tune well). Other verses can be added easily; e.g. God made me, God knows me.

Presentation:
To reinforce the message, when teaching the song introduce it something like this: "We've learnt about how God loves us. That's something that can really make us happy. Let's learn a song that tells us that God loves us."

The leader then sings the song (or even plays it on a tape) a couple of times and then the children join in. You don't need formal accompaniment. You can accompany a song with clapping or handmade percussion instruments (shakers, bells, drums). Alternatively, actions could accompany the song.

The song can be repeated a few times with variety coming from the way it is sung (remember that whenever you're singing the song, you are reinforcing the message). Different ways of singing a song include:
· clap
· clap hands, then knees
· have two parts—divide the children in half; they sing one line each and two lines together
· percussion instruments

Other verses could be added at a later date—if you've hit on a popular song, then other verses can be added to reinforce the message from other lessons.

f. Example for five- to seven-year-olds
Songs that are based on a Bible verse can be written for this age group, and are an ideal way of reinforcing a message. At the time of writing the following song, our Sunday School was studying David, and in particular, 2 Samuel 7.

Bible verse:
"How great you are, O Sovereign LORD! There is no-one like you, and there is no God but you, as we have heard with our own ears." (2 Samuel 7:22)

The song:

Presentation:
This song lends itself well to percussion accompaniment or clapping. For a variation, children could try alternately clapping once on their knees and once with their hands (thus adding to their interest and enjoyment).

g. Leading a children's song
Again there are some basic principles:
- Take time positioning yourself so that you are close to the children to help build rapport. If you have a small group or a young group it is far preferable to sit just in front of them while leading the singing rather than standing. You will appear very, very tall if you are standing in front of pre-schoolers sitting on the floor.
- Take time positioning the group so that each child can see you and you can see them. Don't be afraid to ask the children to move forward or inwards to fill up spaces on the floor. It's far easier to lead children if they are in a tight group than if they are straggled all over the floor with metres between each child!
- In everything you say to direct the children, use short, simple explanations. Don't give long introductions—you'll lose them before you even get started.
- Make it clear when the children are to begin singing. Use hand gestures to lead them, or count them in.
- Maintain eye contact as much as possible—looking around the group as they sing, making them all feel part of the action.
- Be careful of the speed of the song. Make sure that it is not too slow and boring, but not too fast so that they become lost. Watch to see how the children are coping with the speed. If necessary start again—explaining to the children, "I think we need to sing that song a bit faster/slower, don't we!"
- Be enthusiastic and use exaggerated facial expressions. Show that you are enjoying it too! In fact, you will find that your enjoyment is contagious—if you convey that you are having fun then the children will want to join in the fun.
- Variety between active and passive songs is important—some songs are loud and active, while others are quieter. Include a combination and avoid long stretches of inactivity.
- Song sheets should have big, bold type (written in lower case) on large sheets of cardboard, positioned so that everyone can see. Remember that in a group of young children, the song sheets are only for the teachers (and they need to sing loudly!). One way of helping younger children to know the words is to use picture cards.

h. Accompaniment
Accompaniment can vary. The guitar is good because the guitarist can face the children. A piano is a great accompaniment to children's singing, and

if you have both a piano and a pianist then enjoy the privilege!

Accompaniment is not always necessary. Children are adaptable and will enjoy singing however it is done, as long as it is fun. Children can be involved in such a way that they become the accompaniment, such as doing actions, using percussion instruments, and clapping.

Young children, in particular, enjoy percussion instruments. If they are used, it needs to be well controlled. In a large group, at least half the children should have an instrument and then swap (in a small group every child could have one). Children can make some instruments themselves, such as shakers.

i. Teaching a new song

When teaching a new song, the Sunday School teachers should learn it beforehand if possible. Don't teach a new song to young children line by line—you will lose them. It is best if the song leader can sing the song through once and the children can gradually join in on the second and third time through. A longer song could be broken into chunks and only part of the song learnt at one time.

a. Write a list of songs that you frequently sing at Sunday School:

THINK AND DO

b. Now go through them one by one and think about their lyrics:
- *Are they truthful and helpful?*

- *Are there any difficult words, phrases or concepts?*

- *Would the children be able to understand them?*

- *Do the children enjoy singing them?*

- *If you are concerned about the songs that are presently being sung, it would be valuable to talk to the song leader or superintendent.*

6. Conclusion

You will really need to experiment with what is most suitable for your Sunday School. If certain songs or activities result in disruptive behaviour (which will then be unhelpful for the class times) then think of an alternative the following week.

It is not possible for this manual to provide you with a foolproof formula for the group time. Each group of children is different, and each leader is different. Get an idea of what the children enjoy (so they want to come along) and what is most helpful (so the time is used wisely and productively).

There may be some Sunday Schools where a group time is inappropriate. The nature of the hall may not lend itself to a group time or the children may spend some time in church with the adults and then go straight to their classes. If this is the case with your Sunday School, you may want to try different ways of including a song or two in the lesson.

▲ ● ■
THINK

Here are a few things to think about as a teacher sitting with the children in the group time:

- *How can I seat the children in my class so that I am near them?*

- *Am I actively involved in observing and managing the behaviour of the children sitting near me? If not, how can I?*

- *How can I make an effort to learn the words of songs so that I can sing enthusiastically?*

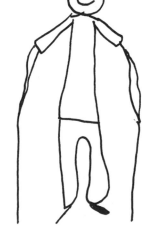

---

1. One example in Australia of a godly, Christian singer who has aimed to produce songs that appeal to children and are biblical with helpful lyrics, is Colin Buchanan. Plainsong Music's *The King, the Snake and the Promise* is also an excellent resource. These resources are available through Matthias Media.

Chapter 11

Safety issues and toilet troubles

In this chapter

1. Safety first

When people are involved in children's ministry on a voluntary basis, like Sunday School, safety issues are often taken lightly. However, in organizations which cater for children on a full-time basis, like pre-schools and schools, safety issues are given considerable attention. Volunteers involved in children's ministry need to realise that the safety of the children is important and needs to be given adequate attention.

I have heard of three separate cases (in a Sunday School and a Bible study creche) where children have either been injured (needing medical attention) or where children have 'escaped' from the hall and been found elsewhere. In one case, two men (not from the church) found a child on the footpath next to a busy road, and were quite abusive towards the carers!

Serious questions arise from this: Are we taking appropriate steps to keep our children safe? What will outsiders and newcomers think of us if safety issues aren't adequately addressed? What would happen to our Sunday School/church if there was an accident in which the Sunday School teachers were found to be negligent? Safety concerns need to be on the agenda of Sunday Schools and churches.

2. What can you do?

Here is a list of suggestions:
- Look around your hall/room and check that it is adequately safe—is there any electrical wiring lying around, are there nails sticking out of furniture or floorboards, are there floorboards missing, are there ladders or unsafe objects in the room? You may want to get a parent who is a handyman to check out your room. If anything in the room is unsafe, ask the appropriate person (your superintendent or minister) to ensure that it is attended to urgently.
- Have procedures in writing for both the parents and the teachers (such as how children are to be dropped off at Sunday School, who is responsible for collecting or returning children after Sunday School).
- If you have an exit that is next to a road or carpark, always have someone supervising it before and after Sunday School.
- You may need to have some safety rules (e.g. always hold the teacher's hand and walk when leaving the hall).
- Keep sharp and potentially unsafe objects, like adult scissors, staplers and split pins, out of reach of the children. On top of a bookshelf or cupboard would be a good location. Make sure that you do cutting for children if they are not able to use scissors proficiently.
- **Never let the children in your class leave your sight**—if they need to go somewhere like the toilet, have someone responsible for taking them there.

- Discourage all forms of climbing and only use chairs for sitting on.
- Be very careful with games. Try to avoid children getting hyped up and silly—that's when accidents may happen. It is possible to play games which are fun yet not too boisterous.
- Have a simple first-aid kit visible in the hall—as much as anything this shows people that you do care and that you have given safety some thought.
- Find out if there is a doctor or nurse who attends church while Sunday School is on (just in case).
- Make sure that you know if any children have a serious medical problem (e.g. epilepsy, a severe reaction to certain foods or even bee stings) which may have implications for Sunday School. This information can be obtained on a Sunday School enrolment form (see chapter 14).
- Talk to your superintendent, or if you are the superintendent, your pastor, about any safety issues that concern you.

A checklist for you to consider and then initiate action...

▲ ● ■
THINK AND DO

Does your Sunday School have.....	yes	no
any unsafe objects in the hall?	☐	☐
a written procedure for dropping off/collecting children?	☐	☐
a safe exit (a gate and a guard)?	☐	☐
safety rules and procedures?	☐	☐
first aid kit?	☐	☐
information regarding children's medical conditions?	☐	☐

3. Toilet troubles

When children first start Sunday School they are usually toilet trained, but in the case of a transition creche class or a young pre-school class, there may be some still in nappies (or some form of training pants); and young children occasionally wet their pants. So here are a few guidelines for classes with children up to 4 years of age:
- Find out from the parents who is/isn't toilet trained, whether there are spare nappies/clothes in a bag, and whether the child will need to go to the toilet.
- Before the story (which you want free of interruptions) offer to take children to the toilet.
- If a young child calls out in a rather urgent voice that they need to do a 'wee-wee'—hurry! They may well be doing it as they speak.
- It's always wise to have someone allocated (and therefore free) to take young children to the toilet—for instance, a second teacher in a team or the superintendent.

- For the sake of being publicly blameless and free of accusation, I would recommend that only females take children to the toilet. Many churches/denominations have policies in these sorts of areas, eg. some denominational guidelines recommend two adults be with the children at all times. This can be for the protection of the adults as well as the protection of the children. Familiarise yourself with your church's policies and any applicable legal requirements.
- Have cleaning supplies (sponge and disinfectant) handy in the Sunday School hall for any accidents.
- If a child does wet their pants, it is not your fault. Young children are learning bladder control and accidents do happen. Try to be relaxed and matter-of-fact about it and reassure the child so that they don't become embarrassed (e.g. "It's OK, we'll just put on some pants from your bag"). The bigger the fuss you make, the more upset they'll be. It may be necessary to call on the child's parents—this can be done discreetly.

Chapter 12

The superintendent

In this chapter

1. What does the superintendent do for:

    The children

    The teachers

    The parents/families

2. A super superintendent's job description

The superintendent is responsible for the smooth running and management of the Sunday School. It is a role requiring organizational skills as well as an understanding of teaching children.

1. What does the superintendent do for...?

a. The children

- Keep and update the roll (with names, contact details and birthdays).
- Remind teachers of children's birthdays.
- Notice if children have been absent for a few weeks and follow it up.
- Be mindful of the children's safety (e.g. guard the entrance to the Sunday School hall at the beginning and end of Sunday School ensuring that no children leave without an appropriate adult, attend to any unsafe aspects of the hall, and so on).
- Welcome new parents and be able to direct new children to the appropriate class.
- First aid and cleaning—not to do it but to make sure that a first aid box is available with band-aids, tissues, disposable gloves, antiseptic, and so on; and to have cleaning supplies on hand for the inevitable spills.

b. The teachers

- Maintain address and phone details.
- Encourage and support them in the task.
- Give them an outline of what's required of them.
- Provide back-up to the teachers by being a key discipline figure that children can be sent to if misbehaving.
- Liaise between the teachers and the church congregation.
- Organise teacher training.
- Coordinate craft supplies (if that is appropriate in your Sunday School context). This would involve keeping a list of supplies needed, as well as re-ordering and distributing them as necessary. Also it would be good to ask parents to bring in recycled supplies from home (e.g. cardboard rolls, egg cartons, tissue boxes, foam vegetable trays, strawberry punnets) and have a carton in the hall as a 'collection depot'.

c. The parents/families

- Liaise between the teachers and parents.
- Organise a copy of the syllabus for parents, and a list of teachers and classes.
- Write letters concerning special events, changes in teachers, and so on, as well as a letter outlining safety issues (e.g. collecting children from Sunday School).

2. A super superintendent's job description

- gate watcher
- welcomer
- roll keeper
- secretary
- facilitator
- disciplinarian
- role model
- problem solver
- encourager
- relief teacher
- teacher training coordinator
- craft coordinator
- first-aid person
- morning tea supervisor

...And you thought you'd be twiddling your thumbs!

More than anything, as a superintendent, you are the leader of the whole Sunday School team. Your positive attitude to the kids, your vision for the importance of teaching them, your enthusiasm and dedication to the task—all these will speak volumes both to the other teachers, and to the parents.

Here is an example of what a superintendent may do on a Sunday:

Greet parents as they arrive.
- Hand out and collect registration forms where appropriate.
- Give a newcomers' booklet to new families.

Keep the roll.
- Maintain an up-to-date list of the classes.
- Have a copy of any rosters [e.g. wash up] and remind teachers.

Keep an eye on the time.
- For example, if there is a group opening session, encourage classes to move to the floor for the opening session at the appropriate time.

Help in the opening session (if you have one).
- Sit at the back to see, greet and direct latecomers so that there is little disruption to the opening session.

Help during class time.
- Be the discipline figure—children may be sent to you by their class teacher.
- Occasionally walk around the hall or room so that children are aware of your presence.
- Take children to the toilet (or, if you are male, arrange for a female

teacher to do so, while you temporarily help out in the teacher's class).
- Set up and distribute morning tea (if you have such a thing).
- Make sure that the bin is visible; have a box for paper recycling if possible.

Stay on duty after class time.
- Be the gate keeper as children leave the hall.
- Ensure that children behave appropriately in the hall while waiting for parents.

▲ ● ■
PRAY

a. The superintendent has an important, and often demanding, role. If that is your role, pray for God's wisdom and strength to persevere in it.

b. If you are not a superintendent, make sure you support your superintendent with words of encouragement as he/she seeks to serve you and the children. Pray for him/her.

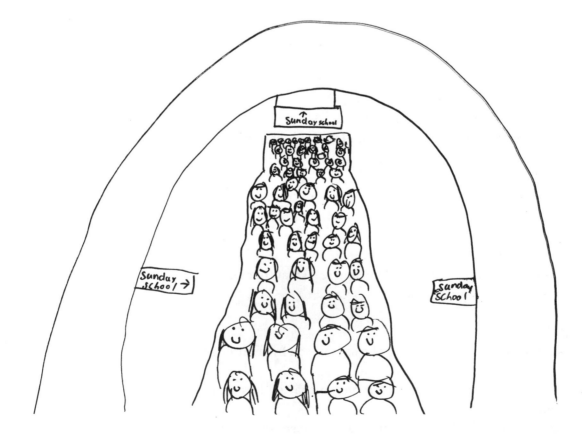

Chapter 13

Training Sunday School teachers

In this chapter

For the trainer

A six-session training course

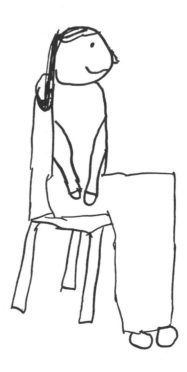

Sunday School teachers are made not born. The demanding task of teaching the Bible to young children is not one which comes naturally, although some churches seem to think it does, judging by the way they throw Sunday School teachers into the job with little or no training. We would never expect someone to be appointed to teach and preach to adults without proper training (usually involving several years of full-time study!). And yet many new Sunday School teachers are left to flounder unaided and untrained. This not only damages the new teacher's confidence and enthusiasm (as he or she struggles to come to terms with the task), but also has obvious effects on the quality of the teaching, and consequently on the children's experience of Sunday School.

A commitment to running a Sunday School means an equal commitment to training and supporting teachers. In many ways, this whole book arose out of the conviction that most churches need to do better in providing training, resources, support and encouragement to Sunday School teachers.

This chapter shows how to use the material in this book as the basis for a six-week basic training course for teachers. Below are outlines for six possible sessions, with notes for the trainer, suggestions for training exercises, and so on. These, of course, are only a guide, and you must feel free to adapt, supplement or change these sessions as your circumstances dictate. Nor is the proposed six-session training course meant to be the start and finish of teacher training. I hope that this book will stimulate you to see many areas in which ongoing evaluation and training should take place, as a regular part of supporting your Sunday School teachers, and helping them to do a better job.

First, however, some general thoughts for the trainer.

1. For the trainer

Who, me?
Firstly, don't fret if you feel inadequate for the job. In particular, don't worry if you are not a trained school teacher. The reality is that very few trained teachers are involved in Sunday School teaching or training (usually because they teach children five days a week and would rather be involved in other ministries on Sunday). So that means that most people who do the training of Sunday School teachers are not professionally qualified teachers and feel inadequate for the task. So you can join the club!

Who should be trained?
Teacher training is valuable for both the new teacher and those who are more experienced teachers. It is beneficial for the experienced teacher to be reminded of the basics of why and how they teach, and to receive some new ideas and resources—it is very easy to get into a 'rut' when teaching.

When?

The six sessions below can be done in a variety of ways. Here are some suggestions:

- Over the course of six weeks—maybe one night a week or on a Sunday after Sunday School.
- Over the course of three weeks—running two sessions per night with a break in the middle.
- Over a weekend (like a camp or houseparty)—with session 1 on Friday night, sessions 2-4 on Saturday and sessions 5-6 on Sunday.
- Over two Saturdays—with sessions 1-3 on the first Saturday, and sessions 4-6 on the second Saturday.

Think about the teachers in your Sunday School and their time available before deciding on the most suitable option for training.

How?

If you have volunteered (or been conscripted!) to train Sunday School teachers, here are a few tips.

Enthusiasm and commitment are more important than experience. Your role is more of a guide than a 'teacher'—helping Sunday School teachers to work through the ideas presented in the first part of this book. And remember that it is God that we are glorifying in our work—pray that God might help you in your preparation and presentation.

Begin by reading this book. The training sessions run parallel with chapters 1-7. Your preparation will basically involve reading each chapter alongside the training session notes for that chapter, and working out how you will conduct each session. Each session has five components:

- Introduction and warm up
- Large group (some input from you)
- Exercise
- Action station
- Homework

With what?

Appendix C contains outlines for each session, either to hand out to trainees or to use as overheads. Feel free to photocopy these outlines as required.

What—again?

It is possible that you will do teacher training again next year. (I realise that you haven't started this year's yet!) I would encourage you to write notes in this book about how effective each session was, as well as any ideas on how to improve them. A few notes scribbled down now will make you all the more prepared and confident next time.

Session 1: The Sunday School teacher

About this session

For this first training session, the trainees will not have read any of the text of the book prior to meeting. The purpose of this session will be to:

· encourage the teachers in their role of Sunday School teaching
· consider together the seriousness of this ministry
· introduce this book and describe how it will be used
· outline the nature of the training sessions, i.e. attendance, homework.

1. Introduction and reflections

· Warmly welcome everyone and ensure that everyone has a copy of this book, plus paper, pen and Bible
· Ask the group: *Who went to Sunday School as a child? What do you remember about it?*

This is a gentle introduction to the whole area of Sunday School teaching. I have found that many people teach Sunday School because they either did go themselves or they didn't!

For those who did go, there are those whose faith really began at Sunday School—they may have fond memories of a particular teacher or a warm feeling as they think of their Sunday School hall or a picnic they went on. They are teaching now because they found Sunday School valuable and want to enable other children to learn about God.

Others who went to Sunday School as a child may have hated it, and are now wanting to teach to provide children with a better experience than they themselves had.

For those adults who never attended Sunday School as a child, many wish that they had, rather than only hearing God's good news in later life. They may have had many turbulent years before becoming a Christian, and they want children to have the opportunity to learn about God before experiencing the hurts/darkness that they have been through.

Your role in encouraging answers to these questions is to help the teachers to see where they are all coming from—to acknowledge the diversity of backgrounds—and to encourage the teachers to think about why they want to teach Sunday School themselves. Which leads us to the next question...

· Ask the group: *Why do you want to teach Sunday School?*
Encourage the teachers to think through their commitment over the next week, and to pray about their commitment to teaching and the children in their care.

2. Large group input: The characteristics of a Sunday School teacher

- In Chapter 1, read aloud the first three paragraphs on page 12, 'Characteristics of a Sunday School teacher'.
- On a board or using Overhead #1 (in Appendix D), list the six points (a-f) under 'Characteristics of a Sunday School teacher'. Briefly discuss each one.

3. Think and pray exercise

This should be done in smaller groups. If you have more than eight trainees, divide into groups of 4-6.

Read 1 Thessalonians 2:17-3:13 and answer the following questions.
- *What was Paul's goal for the Thessalonians?*

- *What was his attitude towards them? How did he feel about them?*

- *How would this sort of attitude be expressed in Sunday School teaching?*

(The trainees will be reading the extra points made from this passage during the week.)

Pray.
- With thankfulness to God for the children in our care.
- For those areas of godliness that we need to work hard on.
- That we follow the model of Paul in ministry.

4. Action Station

This deals with sub-sections 3, 4 and 5 in chapter 1 (pages 17–19). You will obviously need to address the group according to what mix of 'new' and 'experienced' teachers you have. Call the group back together (if they have been split up for Bible study and prayer).

New teachers
- Encourage new teachers—reinforce the fact that all teachers were new sometime.
- If at all possible, plan for new teachers to be observers for at least the first week of Sunday School.
- Then, if possible, enable them to wade into Sunday School teaching gradually and not dive into the deep end, e.g. prepare the visual aid for the first time they say the story.

Experienced teachers
- Encourage them in their role of modelling (modelling how to teach Sunday School to new teachers and modelling a godly life to their class).
- Challenge them to think of ways to strengthen their relationship with the children in their care.

Team teachers
- If you have teams of teachers in the different classes, talk about the different ways to divide up the work, and then split up into your teaching teams to decide who will do what in the following term.
- Make sure that each group appoints a scribe, and that the plan is written down so that each teacher is clear about their role and commitment.
- Tables to help work out the responsibilities for each member of the team are included in the outline in Appendix C.

All teachers
- Discuss your Sunday School, how it operates, who is expected to do what. It would be ideal to have this in writing to work through with the teachers, reminding them of their responsibilities.

5. Homework for next session
- Read chapters 1-3 (N.B. tell the trainees that in the following sessions, there will only be one chapter to read as homework).
- Do the 'think and pray' exercises at the end of chapter 2 and chapter 3.
- Emphasize the importance of punctual attendance and completing the homework.

Session 2: Learning about God at different ages

About this session
For this training session the trainees should have read chapters 1-3. This session will cover the material in chapters 2 and 3, in order to:
- remind the trainees of significant characteristics of each age group
- lay the basic principles behind teaching the Bible to children
- consider together the implications of teaching the children in our care.

1. Introduction and observations
- Warmly welcome everyone and (sorry, but this needs to be done) check whether the trainees have done the required reading. There will probably be all kinds of excuses—from blaming the dog to the garbage collectors—but you need to remind everyone of the importance of teaching children about God and the seriousness with which it should be undertaken. Encourage anyone who has not done the required reading to watch one less TV programme this week and to read the appropriate chapters instead.

- Question for a group mainly comprising of new teachers:
Who knows a two-year-old really well? What can you tell me about them?
  Repeat the question with a four-year-old and a six-year-old.

  These questions have a few purposes:
  - to introduce the subject matter
  - to encourage people to share and interact
  - to have fun—it's hard to talk about children for too long without laughing.

- Question for a group of experienced teachers or teachers who have been at Sunday School for at least one week:
What have you observed about the children in your class?
How long (or short) is their attention span at the moment?

  The purpose of these questions is to:
  - get an idea of how well the teachers are understanding the children in their class (not relevant if they have just started teaching)
  - encourage the trainees to make the connection between what they are reading in the book and the children they are teaching.

2. Large group presentation: Teaching children

Understanding children

- Briefly talk about the important features of each age group and their learning about God—make the trainees realise how simple stories need to be for the age group they are teaching. It is difficult for adults to step down to the level of a child and to remember to use simple vocabulary and concepts. In this part of this session, we are trying to 'open their eyes' to the world of a child.
- To reinforce and summarize the material, you may wish to use Overhead Transparency #2 (in Appendix D) in conjunction with the following visual aids (the notes on the Overhead explain the characteristics that each visual aid reminds us of):
  - Two-year-olds: blanket, bucket
  - Preschoolers (3-4 years): blocks, batman cape (this could just be a piece of black fabric)
  - Infants (5-7 years): books, ball

- Have the different items on a table and refer to them as you go. This will not only help the trainees visualize and remember something about the different age groups, but serve as an object lesson for them in the use of visual aids (note that all the items begin with the letter 'B'—to make them easier to remember).

Teaching the Bible to children

- Discuss the general principles listed in chapter 3 and the HUR principle: **H**ear, **U**nderstand, **R**emember. Briefly discuss the importance of these taking place so that children can learn. Use Overhead #3 (in Appendix D) if you wish.

  These are important points foundational for much of the rest of the book, so we want to reinforce them.

3. Think and pray exercise

- As in session 1, divide into small groups, and discuss your answers to the 'think and pray' exercises at the end chapters 2 and 3 (page 31 and 42).
- Pray

4. Action station

- Get trainees to fill in the table on their outline (in Appendix C, page 192).

5. Homework for next session

- Read chapter 4 and do the exercise for Step 1a on page 46.

Session 3: Discover the message

About this session

For this training session the trainees should have read chapter 4 and done the exercise for Step 1a only. If not, now is the time to get serious about the seriousness of training for Sunday School teaching. Remind them of points from session 1 about commitment, enthusiasm towards the task and a godly model—if we don't care about the children sufficiently to learn how best to teach them, are we in the right ministry? It is now that teachers are showing whether they really are intent on being committed or not.

The purpose of this session is to:
- encourage the teachers to prepare well
- to guide them in the first steps of preparation with an emphasis on starting with the Bible
- provide the trainees with an opportunity to study a passage, following the exercises in the text.

1. Introduction

- Ask the group: *Who has taught a Sunday School lesson? What, to you, was the best thing about it?*
  The number of teachers who have already taught a lesson will depend on your circumstances and the timing of the training sessions. If you have teachers in your midst who have taught a number

of lessons then they can think in general terms about the best thing, to them personally, about teaching a lesson.

Hopefully, one of your trainees will answer that the best thing was seeing the children understand or learn or remember what was taught. If someone obliges with that answer then you can go on to make the point that the preparation of the lesson, particularly in what we say, is important. If no-one obliges with that answer, you will have to say it yourself! If we want the children to remember what we teach them, then we need to make sure that we are giving adequate thought beforehand to what we are teaching them and not just how we are teaching them (i.e. using visual aids or puppets or some 'spectacular production').

2. Large group input: Preparing a lesson

- Briefly summarize the material in the introduction to chapter 4 about the importance of starting with the Bible and its message before going on to plan the lesson with all its various activities. Outline the three steps in the overall process of preparing a lesson, before going on to concentrate on Step 1.
- On a board (or using Overhead #4 in Appendix D) write the three sub-steps outlined in chapter 4 and briefly revise them. Ask the group for their answers to exercise 1a.

3. Now you try: Discover the message

- The bulk of this training session is doing the exercises for Steps 1b and 1c. (Note that these exercises are grouped together in Appendix A on page 182.) This can be done in small groups (preferably grouped with other trainees teaching the same age) or, in the case of a small number of trainees, it can be done with everyone together. It is important for the trainees to write down answers in Appendix A, because this material will be referred to in later sessions.

4. Action Station

- After completing the exercises, discuss and write down how you will make sure that this sort of preparation is always done thoroughly before your lesson.
- Thank God for his Word, and the privilege of teaching it. Pray for diligence and faithfulness in doing so.

5. Homework for next session

- Read chapter 5 and do all the exercises listed *except* the 'Illustrate' exercise at Step 2c (page 66).

Session 4: Plan how to teach the message

About this session

For this training session the trainees should have read chapter 5. The purpose of this session is to:

- help the trainees to go from working out the message to preparing how to present it
- consider various types of visual aids
- work together in preparing the sample passage (Luke 8:22-25) for presentation.

1. Introduction

The purpose of the following questions is to encourage (and in some ways, challenge) the trainees to think about how they will know whether children have learnt what they have been taught. It's a recap of some material covered in session 2.

- Ask those who have taught at least one lesson: *Think back to the last/ last few lessons that you have taught. How effectively have the children:*
  - *heard the message?*
  - *understood the message?*
  - *remembered the message?*

- Ask everyone else: *How will you know whether the children have:*
  - *heard the message;*
  - *understood the message;*
  - *remembered the message;*
  that you have presented in a given lesson?

2. Large group input: Plan how to teach the message

- Use Overhead #3 (in Appendix D) to remind the trainees of the general principles in teaching the Bible to children and the HUR principle: **H**ear, **U**nderstand, **R**emember. Reinforce the importance of these taking place so that children can learn.
- With the above in mind, work quickly through the sub-steps of Step 2: "Plan how to teach the message" (see overhead # 4). At the relevant points, ask the group to give some examples of how they chose to introduce and conclude the Luke 8 story (from their homework).

3. Now you try: Illustrate

- Do the 'Now you try' exercise for Step 2c 'Illustrate' (page 184). Divide into groups of three or four for this activity. You (as the trainer) will need to provide the materials for this exercise.
- If there is time, come back together and have the different groups display their works of art.

4. Action Station

· From what the trainees have learnt from chapter 5, make a summary chart, like the one below. Do this in the large group, with people calling out answers and ideas.

Step 2: Plan how to teach the message		
	THINGS TO REMEMBER	ACTIONS TO TAKE
Introducing the story		
Telling the story		
Illustrating the story		
Concluding the story		

5. For next session

· Read chapter 6 and do the relevant exercises, *except* for the very last one under Step 3b (page 101).

Session 5: Design the overall package

About this session

The purpose of this session is to:

· provide the trainees with the opportunity to conclude their preparation of Luke 8:22-25
· equip the trainees with skills in designing the overall package of a lesson
· help their creative juices to flow and their imaginations to be sparked.

1. Introduction

· Ask the group: *Why do we do activities at Sunday School?*

We want to encourage the trainees to keep thinking through the purpose of things they do at Sunday School. It's so easy to answer "because that's what we've always done" without considering whether it's time to make a few changes and alter some 'traditions'.

· Ask the group about other 'traditional' components of a Sunday School lesson. *Why do we...? Is it time to make some changes?*

For instance, if your Sunday School plays games while waiting for children to arrive and if those games are often wild and silly, is it a tradition to conserve or to change?

2. Large group input: What could you make with this?

· On a table have a selection of 'recycled' items like the following:
  · a cardboard roll
  · a foam tray from vegetable packaging
  · a strawberry punnet
  · an egg carton
  · a tissue box

Pick up one of the items and ask the group to brainstorm ideas on what could be made with it. There could be a scribe listing ideas on an overhead. Continue with each item. Encourage the trainees to be creative and imaginative in their thinking.

3. Now you try: Design the overall package

· Break up into small groups of three or four, and do the 'Now you try' exercise for Step 3b on page 185 (where they design the overall package for the lesson on Luke 8). Again, get them to write their answers in the space provided in Appendix A.

4. Action Station

· Get the teachers for each class or age group to sit down together and draw up a standard overall package that will form the basis of their planning for each week (see Appendix C, page 195). This standard package will be varied and adapted according to the aims of the particular lesson, but having a template to work from helps in developing a routine for the class (which children find helpful).

5. Homework for next session

· Read chapter 7 and do the 'think and pray' exercise on page 112 and the 'think and do' exercise on page 117 (encourage them to bring in their puppets for the next session).

Session 6: Keeping control

About this session

The purpose of this training session is to:

- conclude what the trainees have learnt thus far with a look at discipline, i.e. promoting a helpful learning environment where children can listen and learn
- encourage them to keep learning as teachers, particularly through regular evaluation (so they keep learning from their experiences)
- have some fun, and follow the example set by many children in the enjoyment of chocolate!
- encourage each other in the use of puppets.

1. Introduction

(The following questions assume that your trainees are already involved in some way in Sunday School. If they are not, skip straight to point 2.)

- Ask the group: *How do we discipline children at our Sunday School? How effective is it?*

  Challenge everyone to consider the suitability and effectiveness of present discipline strategies. Do changes need to be made? Are teachers consistent or are some teachers more lenient than others?

- Ask the group: *Are children able to listen and learn at our Sunday School?*

  You may need to remind the teachers of the HUR principle. We're thinking of it now in terms of whether the behaviour of the children, and the class management by teachers, encourage learning or not.

2. Large group input: General principles of discipline

- Show the trainees Overhead #5 (in Appendix D), and discuss the principles briefly.
- Discuss how well each of these principles is followed at your Sunday School, and work out which ones to work on. If your trainees are not yet teaching Sunday School, discuss which ones they think would be most difficult, and why.

3. Action Station

- Either in one large group or in small groups (preferably with those teaching a similar age group together) work through the Discipline Strategy exercise in chapter 7, point 1.d (page 113).

4. Group exercise: Discipline evaluation

- If your trainees are already teaching Sunday School, get them to do some or all of the Discipline evaluation, in chapter 15 (on page 176). If your trainees are not yet teaching, simply point this section out to them, and encourage them to conduct such evaluations after they have been teaching for a term or two.

5. To conclude

- Encourage the trainees to keep on learning, and to use the exercises in the evaluation section to help them become better teachers.
- Congratulate the trainees on finishing the training. Award each participant a chocolate prize! You could even bring in a V.I.P. (very important puppet) to present the awards. Have as much fun as you want—think up some additional awards ('the least punctual', 'the worst artist', 'the most creative puppet-maker', etc.).
- Give everyone the opportunity to display their puppets (that were made for homework). You could have a 'puppet parade'.

And a final note to you, the trainer:

Well done, you have made it. I hope that you found this an encouraging, and helpful, experience. If you'll be doing this training next year and would like to do something a bit differently, make a note of it now so you remember!

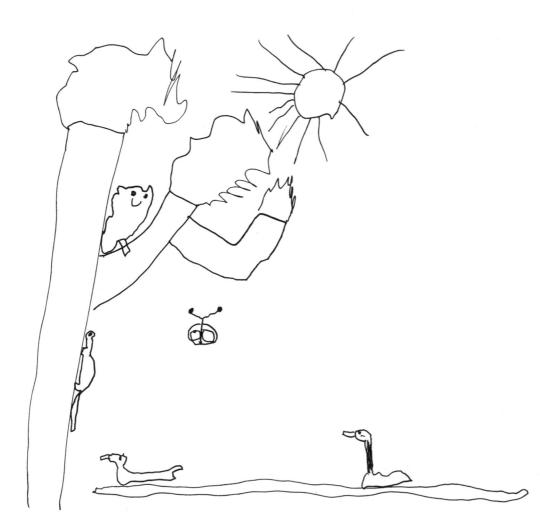

Chapter 14

Getting organized

In this chapter

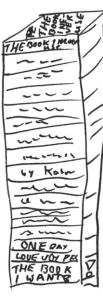

There is a certain amount of administration and organization which is necessary in running an effective Sunday School. Below are some areas that you may or may not have thought of.

1. The roll

Firstly, it is important to have a roll. The superintendent usually keeps the roll for the whole Sunday School, with the class teachers having a list of just their own class.

The information which is necessary for each child is as follows:
· Name
· Address
· Phone number
· Parents' names
· Birthday
· Any important medical information

This information can be obtained by giving the parents a form to fill in soon after they join Sunday School. It is helpful if you can give the parents a printed form so that the Sunday School has the appearance of being organized and thorough. Remember, you will need sensitivity in the case of a child with a single parent or divorced parents.

It is up to you to decide whether you will use the roll to mark attendance. The value of keeping a record of attendance is that you will be aware if a child is absent for a few weeks. The superintendent or minister will be able to decide whether some follow-up needs to be undertaken, like a phone call or visit. One thing to keep in mind, however, is that it is really up to the parents whether or not children come to Sunday School. It would be upsetting to a child if they wanted to come, yet their parents wouldn't allow it. Caution and sensitivity are needed.

2. The syllabus

It is valuable to print the syllabus and give it to the parents. This might be done once a term or once a year. Include the title of each lesson and the Bible reference so that the parents know what the children are learning. Don't abbreviate the Bible references—some parents, especially those who are not Christians, may not understand the abbreviation.

3. Filing lesson notes

If you find that you are making your own visual aids or activity sheets, then it is wise to file them for future reference. You may save yourself much time and effort by devising a simple, convenient filing system and then making the effort to use it.

4. Cards for the children

a. Birthday Cards
One of the best ways for Sunday School teachers to show children that they care about them is to remember their birthdays. As their teacher, you are a significant adult in their lives, and a birthday card from you is especially meaningful. A birthday is an important event to them and a time when they are aware of who cares for them.

So a worthwhile practice is for teachers to write their children's birthdays in a diary at the beginning of the year and send them each a card. The cost of a postage stamp is worth their delight to receive something from their teacher by post. Also, please remember birthdays which fall in the school holidays (especially Christmas holidays). If cards are going to be sent, they need to be sent to everyone.

You needn't purchase cards for young children; a simple handmade card is just as good. Alternatively, you could design a card either by hand or on a computer and then photocopy it.

b. Christmas Cards
Another way of showing children that you remember them is by posting Christmas cards. These have a double value in that they also remind the children about the message of Christmas. It is important that cards are meaningful and free of any unhelpful messages (especially avoid Santa). You may find it easiest to design your own.

5. Organizing special outings

a. Class outings
For older infants children, class outings can be a valuable time to have fun together and get to know each other. Children will take notice that their teachers want to spend time with them.

When choosing a suitable outing there are a few factors to consider. Firstly, safety is important. Avoid any outing that could be potentially dangerous or where you would find it difficult to keep your eye on all the children. Also avoid places which will be expensive for them. Ensure that you have an adequate number of adults present, and that the parents have been given details of the outing in writing and have given their permission. Finally, make sure that you are not trying to be too ambitious. A simple, yet well organised, outing is all that you need.

b. Picnics

Sunday School picnics are popular with children. It's an ideal way to meet the parents and for children, teachers and parents alike to have fun together. Parents will often appreciate you taking the time to go on a picnic with them.

When organising a picnic, here are some important steps:

- Choose a suitable location—one which is easy to find and easy to get to. Also consider safety (is it near a road or water?), shade (if it's hot, will there be shade?), tables (will tables be needed for food?), and a flat area for games. If a picnic is to be held in a large park, you will need to consider how to keep your group contained—both for reasons of safety and a sense of togetherness as a group—as you may end up with little groups of people, even families, sitting by themselves and spread over a large area.
- Decide who is bringing what food and make your arrangements clear to the parents. Do you want them to bring lunch for their family only, or a plate of food for a smorgasbord, or no food at all? Will parents bring drink and cups, or will they be provided?
- Decide on the programme. When will everyone arrive and eat? Will there be games? If so, they need to be thought of, and organised, before the day.
- You may wish to hand out 'lolly bags' or some such thing at the end. An interesting 'tooth-friendly' alternative is a 'craft bag'. You will need a paper bag for each child containing a small number of each of the following (which should be able to be purchased easily and relatively cheaply): plastic drinking straws, paper bags, paper plates, squares of coloured paper, patty cases and maybe some paddle pop sticks, cotton wool balls and/or cheap stickers. Provide a list of ideas of things they could make.

c. Special morning teas

An alternative to a picnic is a morning tea. It can be held in the Sunday School hall, class cubicle or an outside area in the church grounds after Sunday School. It is a simple way of meeting parents informally. Make it clear to the parents whether they need to bring anything.

d. Letters to parents

Whenever you plan an extra activity, write a brief note to the parents a few weeks beforehand. Parents like to be (and need to be) informed.

Never rely on children to relay messages to their parents. They are skilled at forgetting either part or whole messages. To avoid confusion it is worth the effort to put details in writing. It is also important for the parents to receive the note (notes handed to the parent via the children could get dropped on the way, or may end up making an interesting contribution to the washing machine). It is usually best to hand the notes directly to the parents.

A note to parents can also be reinforced by a poster on a notice board or a notice in the church bulletin.

6. A Sunday School information booklet

Here's an excellent idea—being able to hand out a booklet to new parents explaining about the Sunday School (how it is run, what the children do, etc.). It would show new parents that you are well organized and that you expect newcomers. They would feel welcomed and quickly understand how everything works.

Such a booklet is also a useful resource for existing parents. If you were sufficiently organized, you could even produce a new edition at the beginning of each year, setting out the term dates, the syllabus, the dates for any picnics or morning teas, as well as information about the goals, norms and expectations of Sunday School.

It doesn't need to be a world-class production. If it is written clearly and laid out logically, it will do its job.

The only problem with this otherwise excellent idea is how easily it doesn't happen! Somehow producing such a booklet is the kind of non-urgent but very useful thing that always seems to get delayed, put off and eventually shelved. My suggestion is to start small—a few stapled pages that actually exist is better than a 20-page booklet that never gets off the drawing board.

7. A Sunday School registration card

This may sound very formal, but having a registration card is simply a way of updating your roll as new children join the Sunday School. This can be filled out by parents of new children maybe on their second visit, as this shows their attendance is more than just a one-off visit.

See a sample of a registration card on the next page.

8. Samples

Sunday School Registration Card

To help us run a caring, effective and safe Sunday School, please supply us with the following details for your child:

FIRST NAME: _____

SURNAME: _____ M/F

PARENTS NAMES: (Mother) _____ (Father) _____

ADDRESS: _____

_____ Home phone: _____

DATE OF BIRTH: __ / __ / __

☐ Year 2   ☐ Year 1   ☐ Kindergarten   ☐ Commencing school in _____ (eg. 2001)

SPECIAL NEEDS OR OTHER THINGS WE SHOULD KNOW (eg. allergies, asthma):

_____

_____

_____

Invitation

St. John's Sunday School

Dear parents,

On Sunday_____

there will be a
Sunday School picnic
for the families of the Sunday School.

Location:_____

Time: *from____to____*

Please bring sandwiches for your family.
Drinks and cakes will be provided.

N.B. Please remember a picnic rug, hats and sunscreen.

Chapter 15

Evaluation

In this chapter

1. Why evaluate

It is unwise to teach a class for a whole year before you evaluate what you're doing. Ideally, evaluation should be an ongoing process, but a conscious effort should probably be made once a term.

Evaluation is important because each teacher, child and class of children are different. So although the material may not differ from class to class, the effectiveness of it may vary greatly. The key to evaluation is understanding what has and hasn't worked well so that you can try to do more of what has worked well and less of what hasn't. There's no point making the same mistakes over and over without learning from them. Remember: teaching is a continual learning process. It can get a little depressing when it looks like you have a mountain of things to learn, but if you focus on what has been effective there's light ahead!

A planned approach to evaluation is an important step in running a successful Sunday School.

2. What to evaluate

It is valuable to evaluate:
- the content of the lessons
- the teaching techniques
- the effectiveness of the lessons
- the behaviour of the class

The best way to do this is simply to list all of the relevant elements of Sunday School teaching, as in the evaluation sheet at the end of this chapter (with a few variations according to your situation). Teachers should go through the list writing comments about what has and hasn't worked well.

3. How to evaluate

a. Individually

Firstly, evaluation needs to be done individually. For those who teach a class by themselves, then initial evaluation will have to be individual. For those who work with a partner or team, it is still best for each teacher to fill out an evaluation sheet individually before discussing it. Each teacher will view things differently, so it is ideal to get these differing viewpoints before trying to change anything.

When filling out the evaluation sheet it is important to be honest. We all find it difficult to admit our failings. Yet if we try to cover up our problems we will not be able to make improvements. One of the most difficult areas to be honest about may be the behaviour of the class. It takes courage to admit that a group of young children can be difficult to control!

We also need to be balanced in our viewpoints. Don't just look for negative things. Make sure that the positive is also noted, celebrated and continued.

b. With others

Now it's getting harder. Once each class teacher has filled out their evaluations, it is time to discuss the results. Those who work in a team of teachers in one class obviously need to discuss their evaluations, and jointly come up with a plan for improvement. Those who teach on their own will find it helpful to meet with someone else to discuss their evaluation sheet—perhaps the superintendent or another teacher would be suitable. It is helpful to get an objective opinion and ideas.

Of course, in this whole process, honesty, sensitivity and love are important. Critical comments need to be made carefully. If you teach with another teacher or team of teachers, then you will need to reach conclusions together from your evaluation sheets. Again, share your various viewpoints honestly and in love. Remember that you are teaching as a team and need to be helping each other in that task. It may well be that you will realise that the team will work most effectively if you do things quite differently. This may be difficult to acknowledge.

c. Identify target areas

Evaluation needs to be purposeful. It is of no value to spend time in evaluation without identifying specific areas which need to be worked on. So this is where the next sheet entitled 'Target Areas and Strategies' comes in (at the end of this chapter). Once you have discussed your evaluation sheet with another teacher/s, you need to fill in this next sheet together.

Based on the information gained from the evaluation sheets, the class teacher/s need to decide on a few specific areas which need changing. It is important to be specific. General comments will achieve little action. By identifying specific areas that need changing you will be able to be clear in your mind as to what you need to spend more time on.

It is suggested that you decide on three areas which could be improved. You may not be able to think of three—great! Things must be going very well. Alternatively, you may think of more than three. In that case, I would suggest that you try to decide on the three most important areas. You can't change everything at once, and it is far preferable to have a manageable list which will lead to change than to be swamped by everything and do nothing.

Here are examples of some sets of three target areas:
- i. visual aids (need to be more effective)
  ii. prayer (we need to do it more regularly)
  iii. instructions (need to be improved)

- i. introductions (presently don't exist and are needed)
  ii. story telling (need to work on technique)
  iii. discipline (needs to be more consistent)
- i. activities (children find them boring)
  ii. question time (we need one)
  iii. organization (need to be better organized)

d. Think of strategies

Deciding on your target areas is the first step towards change. The next step is to think of strategies for working on each target area. You need to determine how you are going to implement change. Specific, practical strategies are needed. Identifying the target areas helps in determining what needs to be changed. Thinking of strategies is determining how you are going to make the changes.

So let's look back at the first example of target areas and think of strategies which could be used for each:

i. **Target area**: visual aids (need to be more effective)
   Strategy:
   - read any available material which will provide examples of various visual aids (e.g. chapter 5 of this book)
   - write a list of suitable visual aids for your class
   - read each week's story early in the week and spend a few days thinking of and preparing a suitable visual aid
   - aim for variety—especially try to use 3-dimensional aids and puppets
ii. **Target area**: prayer (we need to do it more regularly)
    Strategy:
    - aim to pray every week
    - begin by praying for a few weeks after the story (about things that come out of the story)
    - then try praying at a different time, asking children to contribute prayer points
    - then try involving the children in prayer (at first they could just say a word e.g. "Thank you God for...")
iii. **Target area**: instructions (need to be improved)
     Strategy:
     - decide which class teacher will be responsible for giving which instructions
     - aim to give all instructions while the children are seated and attentive
     - for the first few weeks, when preparing the activity, write step by step instructions to remind you of what you need to say to the children (ensure that they are sufficiently clear and specific)

One point needs to be made here. The strategies which you work out need to be realistic. You have to be able to work within your time and energy limits. You may find it helpful to think of short- and long-term strategies. For example, the final point under c. (to write down specific instructions) is a short-term measure to help you get used to giving good instructions. If you did this every week it would be exhausting and time consuming. On the other hand, the example of aiming to pray every week is intended as long term. Time needs to be set aside each week to give this thought and preparation.

It is valuable to write your strategies where they can be referred to later in the term as a reminder.

e. Prayer

An important part of the evaluation process is prayer. We need God's help in determining what changes should be made and how to make them. If you teach in a team and do the above evaluation process each term, it would be a valuable opportunity to discuss prayer points for your class. If you are having difficulties in a particular area of your teaching, ask your fellow teachers for prayer support. If you teach by yourself, then find someone else who could pray for you. Prayer is an important part of ministry and makes us realise that we can only make effective changes with God's help.

4. Evaluating discipline

If you have a discipline problem in your class, the best place to start is to analyse the problem yourself. Try to work out what the specific problem is, how it comes about, who the main offenders are, how you deal with it, and so on.

If you teach in a team, the next step is to share your thoughts with your fellow teachers. If you teach by yourself, then find someone else to talk to. Another teacher or the superintendent could be approached.

A special 'discipline evaluation' sheet is included below to help analyse your problem and come up with some solutions.

NB: The Evaluation sheets can be downloaded as PDF files from the Matthias Media website, for easier printing or for email distribution to teachers.

http://www.matthiasmedia.com.au/TGISB/

Evaluation Sheet

COMMENTS

	POSITIVE	CRITICAL

Content of the lessons

- motivation/introduction

- story

- visual aids

- activities

- conclusion

- discussion/question time

- prayer

- memory verses/action rhymes

- news time

Teaching technique

- organisation/preparation

- discipline

- relationship (rapport) with the children

- instructions given

- use of voice

- eye contact

Effectiveness of the lessons

- attention of children

- understanding of the lesson

- memory of previous week's lesson

Behaviour of the class

- is the behaviour of your class acceptable?

- are there any problem areas?

- if so, work through the discipline evaluation sheet

Target areas and Strategies

1. Discuss your evaluation sheets with your fellow teacher/s.

_____

_____

2. Decide on three areas which you both/all feel could be improved this term:

a. _____

_____

b. _____

_____

c. _____

_____

_____

3. Think of strategies for working on each:

a. _____

_____

b. _____

_____

c. _____

_____

4. What could you be praying for your class this term?

_____

_____

Discipline Evaluation Sheet

1. Assess

Think about your class. Are there any discipline problems? If so, what are they? Be specific and list up to three main problems:

a. _____

_____

b. _____

_____

c. _____

_____

2. Analyse

Analyse each problem by thinking through why it exists, how it develops and how you respond to it. Use the 'Discipline Analysis Questions' (next page) for help.

a. _____

_____

b. _____

_____

c. _____

_____

3. Act

Now decide on the appropriate steps to minimize the above problems. Read the 'Discipline Action Suggestions' for ideas. Be specific in detailing the steps you will take:

a. _____

_____

b. _____

_____

c. _____

_____

_____

To help you fill out the Discipline Evaluation Sheet, the pages that follow contain:
· discipline analysis questions
· discipline action suggestions

Reproduced from *THEIR GOD IS SO BIG: Teaching Sunday School to young children*

Discipline Analysis Questions

The following questions may be helpful in getting you to think about your specific problem. The aim of these questions is to think specifically and try to narrow the problem down as much as possible.

Your teaching method
- Do the children know the difference between acceptable and unacceptable behaviour in your class?
- Are you consistent in your treatment of the children? If you teach in a team, are the teachers consistent with each other?
- Do you ever show favouritism?
- Are you firm?
- How effectively do you notice and encourage positive behaviour?
- How do you react when a child begins misbehaving? What effect does your reaction have?
- Do you have any class rules? If so, are they effective? Are there too many? Or too few?

The class
- When are the children most likely to misbehave? Why do you think this is? Does anything set them off?
- Is one particular child the 'ringleader' when it comes to misbehaviour?
- Does he/she have a strong influence on any one child? If so, do they sit together? Are they often opposite each other?
- Are the children always occupied during the lesson?
- How is the class seated for the story/activity?
- Where do the teachers sit in relation to the children?

An individual
- When is he/she naughty? Does something set him/her off?
- In what ways is he/she naughty?
- Is he/she hyperactive?
- Is he/she trying to seek attention? Any idea why?
- Is he/she keeping up with the class? Does he/she have any learning problems?
- On the other hand, is he/she particularly bright and easily bored?
- Does he/she respect you as a teacher? Other authority figures?
- What influences do other children have on him/her? Who does he/she sit with? (Look for positive influences as well as negative ones).

Discipline Action Suggestions

- If you have a team of teachers make sure that one teacher is clearly in charge each week.
- Assign one teacher the task of 'observer' each week to ensure that all the children are being watched and no-one misbehaves unnoticed.
- Write a few class rules and be consistent in adhering to them.
- Separate trouble-makers who sit together.
- Ensure that a teacher sits next to the 'ringleader'.
- Use the superintendent as a disciplinary figure. Never feel embarrassed if you need to send children to him/her.
- Speak to parents if you feel they are unaware of a particular problem. Parents can be very supportive and helpful by having a 'little chat' to their children before they arrive at Sunday School.
- Introduce more variety between active and passive activities.
- Provide a teacher-directed opportunity for children to release energy, wriggle and squirm.
- Lower your expectations of how long the children can sit and concentrate, and plan accordingly.
- Actively use positive reinforcement to praise appropriate behaviour in difficult children.
- Think of a series of threats to use when children misbehave and be consistent in applying them.
- Have a more structured routine so that children clearly know what is happening when; this limits their opportunities for getting up to mischief.
- Keep things moving and always ensure the children are occupied (have something for quick workers to do when they have finished).
- Change seating arrangements for the story time so that the children will find it easier to concentrate (ensure that they are able to see you, are not looking elsewhere and are as comfortable as possible).
- Take discipline more seriously; you want to give every child the opportunity to hear the story and learn more about God.

   Reproduced from *THEIR GOD IS SO BIG: Teaching Sunday School to young children*

Chapter 16

Conclusion

In conclusion, I would personally like to encourage you in your ministry with children by referring to Romans 12:11: "Never be lacking in zeal, but keep your spiritual fervour, serving the Lord".

It's easy to lose our zeal, particularly in children's work. It's tiring, and at times frustrating and discouraging. It is often a difficult task because children are too young to appreciate the valuable ministry you are offering them. Children can appear far more interested in misbehaving than learning about God. So it's easy to question our involvement.

Yet we need to remind ourselves that children are precious. Childhood years are a wonderful time to build foundations. In a seemingly godless world we can help these young minds see that it's actually a God-filled and God-created world. We can help them see God as a reality and not as a swear word.

I hope that this book has been, and will continue to be, helpful in your Sunday School teaching. If you realise that you need to make changes, take time to pray, think, and plan before you act. Children need time and warning to adjust to new routines and changes. And adults do too! Don't have too high expectations of yourself. It probably would be best to make changes gradually so that you are not attempting too much in one go.

"May God… equip you with everything good for doing his will, and may he work in us what is pleasing to him, through Jesus Christ, to whom be glory for ever and ever. Amen" (Heb 13:21).

Appendix A

Now you try

The exercises below are those referred to in chapters 4-6. They take you through the process of preparing a sample lesson on Luke 8:22-25.

Step 1: Discover the message

a. Select
Passage: Luke 8:22-25

b. Understand
- Read the passage
- Underline any difficult words, phrases or concepts.

> [22] One day Jesus said to his disciples, "Let's go over to the other side of the lake." So they got into a boat and set out.
> [23] As they sailed, he fell asleep. A squall came down on the lake, so that the boat was being swamped, and they were in great danger.
> [24] The disciples went and woke him, saying, "Master, Master, we're going to drown!" He got up and rebuked the wind and the raging waters; the storm subsided, and all was calm.
> [25] "Where is your faith?" he asked his disciples. In fear and amazement they asked one another, "Who is this? He commands even the winds and the water, and they obey him."

- Look up the passage in your own Bible so that you can see the context.

- Is the passage addressed to a particular situation or audience?

- What are the main ideas or themes?

- What don't I understand?

- Can I find any helpful cross-references?

- What is the passage about? Write the main point of the passage:

                    Reproduced from *THEIR GOD IS SO BIG: Teaching Sunday School to young children*

c: **Prepare**

Passage: Luke 8: 22-25.

- Choose an age group that you will prepare the lesson for: pre-school (3-4 years old) or infants (5-7 years old).

- Referring to your notes from '1b: Understand', write out the main message you would want to teach your class.

- Now write out the passage (for your age group) simplifying the difficult words, phrases and concepts.

Step 2: Plan how to teach the message

a: Introduce
- Referring to the main message and simplified story (above), work out how you would introduce the story to your chosen age group.

c: Illustrate
- Using the following materials, make a simple visual aid for telling your story (on Luke 8:22-25) to your chosen age group:
    - pieces of cardboard (A4 size is fine)
    - coloured paper
    - fabric scraps (if possible)
    - cotton wool
    - patty cases
    - black pen
    - scissors
    - glue

d: Conclude
- Work out how you will conclude your story on Luke 8:22-25. Write out your conclusion:

- Write down two questions you can ask to check whether your class has understood the story:

Step 3: Design the overall package

a: Select other components

- From the ideas presented in chapter 6, devise an activity for your chosen age group. Write a description of the activity and how it would be made.

- Now write down the step-by-step instructions you would give to your class to complete the activity.

b: Design the package

- Design the overall format of your lesson on Luke 8:22-25, drawing on the various components listed in chapter 6.

Appendix B

Lesson preparation summary

For your convenience, the following page contains a summary of the method outlined in chapters 4-6 for preparing a Sunday School lesson. Feel free to photocopy this summary and keep it handy when doing your preparation.

The following page can also be downloaded as PDF files from the Matthias Media website, for easier printing or for email distribution to teachers.

http://www.matthiasmedia.com.au/TGISB/

Preparing a lesson

Step 1: Discover the message

a. Select

b. Understand
- Read the passage
- Identify any difficult words, phrases or concepts.
- Is the passage addressed to a particular situation or audience?
- What are the main ideas or themes?
- What don't I understand?
- Can I find any helpful cross-references?
- What is the passage about? Write the main point of the passage.

c. Prepare
- What is the main message I want to teach my class?
- Simplify the passage for your class.

Step 2: Plan how to teach the message

a. Introduce
- How will you gain their interest and attention?

b. Tell
- Will you learn the story? Read it?
- Practise.

c. Illustrate
- Visual aids, puppets, models etc.

d. Conclude
- Work out your conclusion, application, questioning.

Step 3: Design the overall package

a. Select other components
- Activities, action rhymes, memory verses, prayer, news time

b. Design the package

Appendix C

Outlines for Sunday School training sessions

On the following pages are outlines corresponding to the six-session teacher training course suggested in chapter 13. Please feel free to reproduce these outlines in whatever form best suits your purpose—e.g. as handouts for trainees, or as overhead transparencies.

The following pages can also be downloaded as PDF files from the Matthias Media website, for easier printing or for email distribution to teachers.

http://www.matthiasmedia.com.au/TGISB/

Sunday School Training
Session 1: The Sunday School teacher

1. Introduction and reflections

2. The characteristics of a Sunday School teacher

a. _____

_____

b. _____

_____

c. _____

_____

d. _____

_____

e. _____

_____

f. _____

3. Think and pray exercise
1 Thessalonians 2:17-3:13

- What was Paul's goal for the Thessalonians?

- What was his attitude towards them? How did he feel about them?

- How would this sort of attitude be expressed in Sunday School teaching?

     Reproduced from *THEIR GOD IS SO BIG: Teaching Sunday School to young children*

Pray
- With thankfulness to God for the children in our care.
- For those areas of godliness that we need to work hard on.
- That we follow the model of Paul in ministry.

4. Action station

New teachers

Experienced teachers

Team teaching

On page 18, there are listed five ways (numbered i-v) in which a team of teachers can divide the workload. If you choose method i, use a table like that below to work out who will take responsibility for which weeks.

Term dates										
TEACHERS	4/2	11/2	18/2	25/2	4/3	11/3	18/3	25/3	1/4	8/4
Jo	x					x				
Jan		x						x		
John				x	x				x	
Julian			x				x			x

If you choose one of the methods labelled ii-v, use a table like the one below to divide up the responsibilities each week:

Term dates										
	4/2	11/2	18/2	25/2	4/3	11/3	18/3	25/3	1/4	8/4
Leader	John	Jan	Jo	Julian	John	Jan	Jo	Julian	John	Jan
Story	Jan	Jo	Julian	John	Jan	Jo	Julian	John	Jan	Jo
Activity	Jo	Julian	John	Jan	Jo	Julian	John	Jan	Jo	Julian
Memory verse	Julian	John	Jan	Jo	Julian	John	Jan	Jo	Julian	John

5. Homework for next session
- Read chapters 1-3.
- Do the 'think and pray' exercises at the end of chapter 2 (page 31) and chapter 3 (page 42).

Sunday School Training
Session 2: Learning about God at different ages

1. Introduction and observations

2. Teaching children
Understanding children
- Two-year-olds

- Pre-schoolers

- Infants

Teaching the Bible to children

3. Think and pray exercise

4. Action station
Fill out the following table:

	WHAT I HAVE LEARNT	HOW I'M GOING TO ACT AS A RESULT
General principles of teaching children		
Important characteristics of two-year-olds		
Teaching the Bible to two-year-olds		
Important characteristics of pre-schoolers		
Teaching the Bible to pre-schoolers		
Important characteristics of infants children		
Teaching the Bible to infants children		

5. Homework for next session
- Read chapter 4 and do the 'think and do' exercise on page 46.

Reproduced from *THEIR GOD IS SO BIG: Teaching Sunday School to young children*

Sunday School Training
Session 3: Discover the message

1. Introduction

2. Preparing a lesson
Step 1: Discover the message

-

-

-

3. Now you try: Discover the message

4. Action station
- How will you make sure this sort of preparation is done each week?

- Thank God for his word and the privilege of teaching it.
- Pray for diligence and faithfulness.

5. Homework for next session
- Read chapter 5 and do all the exercises listed.

Sunday School Training
Session 4: Plan how to teach the message

1. Introduction
How effective is your HUR?
How will you know?

2. Step 2: Plan how to teach the message

a _____

_____

b _____

_____

c _____

_____

d _____

_____

3. Now you try: Illustrate

4. Action station
· Summarizing what we've learned.

Step 2: Plan how to teach the message		
	THINGS TO REMEMBER	ACTIONS TO TAKE
Introducing the story		
Telling the story		
Illustrating the story		
Concluding the story		

5. Homework for next session
· Read chapter 6 and do the relevant exercises, except for 'now you try' on page 101.

   Reproduced from *THEIR GOD IS SO BIG: Teaching Sunday School to young children*

Sunday School Training
Session 5: Design the overall package

1. Introduction
Why do we do what we do?

2. What could you make with this?

3. Now you try: Design the overall package

4. Action station
Design your standard package:

1. _____
2. _____
3. _____
4. _____
5. _____
6. _____
7. _____
8. _____

5. Homework for next session
· Read chapter 7 and do the 'think and pray' exercise on page 112 and 'think and do' exercise on page 117.

Sunday School Training
Session 6: Keeping control

1. Introduction
How effective is our discipline?
Are children able to listen and learn?

2. Principles of discipline

3. Action station
Discipline strategy exercise

4. Discipline evaluation

5. To conclude

Appendix D

Overhead transparencies for training sessions

The following pages can be photocopied onto overhead transparency sheets and used during the training sessions.

The following pages can also be downloaded as PDF files from the Matthias Media website, for easier printing.

http://www.matthiasmedia.com.au/TGISB/

Characteristics of a Sunday School teacher

a. A godly model

b. Committed

c. Caring

d. Prepared

e. Enthusiastic

f. Prayerful

Understanding Children

Two-year-olds

Blanket—they need security and routine, and may bring a 'security blanket' with them.

Bucket—they are exploring and learning rapidly about their world and play alongside rather than 'with' each other.

Pre-school (3-4 years)

Blocks—playing is learning, learning is playing; they are busy playing, learning, building, exploring.

Batman cape—they are imaginative and creative.

Infants (5-7 years)

Books—school, learning to read, success and failure

Ball—peers more important, play socially

OVERHEAD #3

Teaching the Bible to children

General principles

a. Prepare well

b. Teach accurately and faithfully

c. Teach prayerfully

d. Teach meaningfully

e. Teach so children learn

The HUR principle of learning

Hear

Understand

Remember

Preparing a lesson

Step 1: Discover the message

a. Select

b. Understand

c. Prepare

Step 2: Plan how to teach the message

a. Introduce

b. Tell

c. Illustrate

d. Conclude

Step 3: Design the overall package

a. Select other components

b. Design the package

General principles of discipline

i. Be in control of your class:

- be observant and notice what's happening
- be firm
- expect respect

ii. Be loving.

iii. Aim to prevent rather than punish.

iv. Use positive reinforcement.

v. Set clear guidelines for acceptable and unacceptable behaviour:

- be consistent and fair in adhering to these
- think beforehand of what threats you will make and when
- remember to do what you say you'll do
  (don't make empty threats)
- have class rules if appropriate

vi. Be well organized:

- Know what you want to do when
- Yet be flexible and adapt to their behaviour (provide concentration breaks if necessary)
- Keep things moving

vii. Be responsible.

MATTHIAS MEDIA

Who are we?

Ever since 'St Matthias Press and Tapes' first opened its doors in 1988, under the auspices of St Matthias Anglican Church, Centennial Park, in Sydney, our aim has been to provide the Christian community with products of a uniformly high standard—both in their biblical faithfulness and in the quality of the writing and production.

Now known as Matthias Media, we have grown to become an international provider of user-friendly resources, with Christians of all sorts using our Bible studies, books, Briefings, audio cassettes, videos, training courses—you name it.

Buy direct from us and save

If you order your Matthias Media resources direct from us, you not only save time and money, you invest in more great resources for the future:

- you save time—we usually despatch our orders within 24 hours of receiving them
- you save money—our normal prices are better than other retailers' discounts (plus if you order in bulk, you'll save even more)
- you help keep us afloat—because we get more from each sale, buying from us direct helps us to stay alive in the difficult world of publishing.

Please call us for a free catalogue of all our resources or visit our website.

1800 814 360
or in Sydney:
(02) 9663 1478

Reply Paid 225,
Kingsford
NSW 2032

FAX
(02) 9662 4289
(pay by credit
card or invoice)

Email:
sales@matthiasmedia.com.au

Internet:
www.matthiasmedia.com.au

Postcard from Palestine

POSTCARD
— FROM —
PALESTINE

A hands on guide to
reading and using the Bible

God has a message for us—a message about himself and us and the world and everything that's important in life. The only trouble is that this message was originally delivered several thousand years ago in Palestine.

Postcard from Palestine shows you how God's word, originally delivered so long ago and so far away, is still addressed to us today.

Author Andrew Reid provides examples and practical 'hands on' exercises, so that you can see how to make the most of reading the Bible, and then try it for yourself.

In this new edition, *Postcard from Palestine* is simpler and shorter, and can be completed in a weekly study group in just 8 sessions.

Andrew Reid is well-known throughout Australia as an evangelical leader and Bible teacher. He was formerly the national director of the Australian Fellowship of Evangelical Students (AFES).

1800 814 360
or in Sydney:
(02) 9663 1478

Reply Paid 225,
**Kingsford
NSW 2032**

FAX
(02) 9662 4289
(pay by credit
card or invoice)

Email:
sales@matthiasmedia.com.au

Internet:
www.matthiasmedia.com.au

Extra Notes

Extra Notes

Extra Notes

Extra Notes

Extra Notes